Digital Vortex Survival Guide

Behaviors, Digital Media, & the Brain

Julie Doan, RN and Christie Walsh

This workbook belongs to:

Denise & Dutch Bergman

May God Bless you and your ministry!

Love & Blessings

Christie Walsh
&
Michael Walsh

Digital Vortex Survival Guide: Behaviors, Digital Media, and the Brain

By Julie Doan, RN and Christie Walsh

Copyright © 2017 by Julie Doan and Christie Walsh

Scriptures taken from the New King James Version®. Copyright © 1982 by Thomas Nelson. Used by permission. All rights reserved.

Scripture quotations from The Authorized (King James) Version. Rights in the Authorized Version in the United Kingdom are vested in the Crown. Reproduced by permission of the Crown's patentee, Cambridge University Press.

Published and distributed by F.E.P. International, Inc.: www.fepint.org

Published for Real Battle Ministries: www.realbattle.org

Real Battle Ministries is a non-profit organization under section 501(c)(3) of the United States Internal Revenue Code.

Printed in the United States of America

For information write F.E.P. International, Inc.: www.fepint.org

ISBN 978-1-935576-05-1

Table of Contents

Acknowledgements

I would like to give thanks and praise to my savior, Jesus Christ. Without Him, nothing is possible. I want to thank my amazing family for their love and support. Andrew, you always push me to do more for Real Battle Ministries. Nick, Kate, and Emily, I look at you all, and I feel revitalized to fight the Real Battles worth fighting for.

- Julie Doan

This has been an amazing experience. I need to acknowledge God for waking me up and giving me this opportunity to work with so many great people. I would like to thank my loving husband and children who helped me in many ways to put these materials together in a form that would help as many people as possible. I thank my father who was very helpful by contributing scriptural references, as only a dad and minister can do. I thank my mom who always helps with her loving support. I also thank Bob Bland of Teen Missions International and their entire staff for supporting this cause and offering their insight from working with thousands of teens. Finally, I thank Dr. Andrew and Julie Doan, for their scientific and spiritual leadership and for founding Real Battle Ministries, without which none of this would have been possible. This has truly been an experience that has exemplified Romans 8:28; We know all things work together for good for those who love God, to those who are called according to His purpose.

- Christie Walsh

Julie Doan, RN

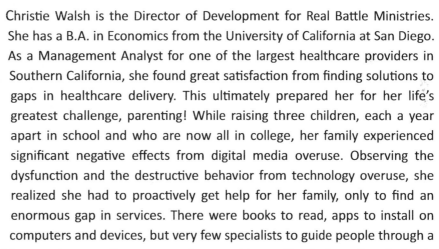

Julie Doan is a registered nurse who has an interest in child development, neuroscience, and digital media addictions. She is married to Dr. Andrew Doan (M.D., Ph.D., neuroscientist and researcher in addictive behaviors). Dr. Andrew and Julie Doan research digital media addictions and methods to help families thrive by overcoming digital media overuse. With her husband, they founded Real Battle Ministries where she and her husband have given talks around the world about the problems associated with digital media overuse. She is a highly-demanded speaker with near perfect 5-star Verified Reviews®. Dr. Andrew & Julie Doan have over 95,000 followers on Facebook. They also have over 550,000 followers on their Christian Recovery Resource Facebook page where they evangelize, teach, and share about the consequences with excessive digital media use. Julie is a mother of two college students and one pre-teen girl. She is currently pursuing a career as a life coach.

Christie Walsh

Christie Walsh is the Director of Development for Real Battle Ministries. She has a B.A. in Economics from the University of California at San Diego. As a Management Analyst for one of the largest healthcare providers in Southern California, she found great satisfaction from finding solutions to gaps in healthcare delivery. This ultimately prepared her for her life's greatest challenge, parenting! While raising three children, each a year apart in school and who are now all in college, her family experienced significant negative effects from digital media overuse. Observing the dysfunction and the destructive behavior from technology overuse, she realized she had to proactively get help for her family, only to find an enormous gap in services. There were books to read, apps to install on computers and devices, but very few specialists to guide people through a process of resolving the problem and preventing more serious problems. Dr. Andrew Doan's book, "Hooked on Games", was instrumental in connecting the neurochemistry processes stimulated by digital media with destructive, self-limiting behaviors. Consulting with specialists and thought leaders in this new and burgeoning field provided the tools to convince her family to limit digital media use. While spending 10 years dedicated to studying the issue and finding solutions for her family, she realized this is an issue that is affecting the best and brightest of our youth, is a worldwide phenomenon, spans every age group and must be made known. Together, Julie Doan, Christie Walsh and Real Battle Ministries have developed this workbook to educate and empower people to help win this very Real Battle!

Endorsements

Julie and Christie convey complex neuroscience and brain development in an understandable way. The workbook is well-designed with great graphics to help teens and parents understand how behaviors and digital media affect the brain. The book is timely and brilliant. All families and teens need this book, at least the ones who want to succeed in the digital age and avoid being sucked into a digital vortex! - **Aaron Tabor, M.D., Founder of Jesus Daily® with over 30 million Facebook followers.**

Digital Natives are into technology. They're in deep. So, why is that a problem? The "Digital Vortex Survival Guide" is a powerful resource for parents, teachers and all caring people who are concerned about an entire tech-savvy generation. The authors have crafted an easy-to-understand guide that explains how the effects of excessive media tech usage impact the brain of developing teens. This book will help you be informed, stay alert and know what it takes to live a balanced life in an overstimulated world. - **Linda Mintle, Ph.D. Chair, Behavioral Health, Liberty University College of Osteopathic Medicine; Author, "Raising Healthy Kids in an Unhealthy World."**

This workbook is a refreshing and substantial combination of the truth in the word of life, neuroscience excellence, neural pruning, insights into brain programming, and strategies for achieving optimal health. Doan & Walsh do a masterful job in identifying the unhealthy and addictive behaviors that program our brains and provide discussion questions to reprogram or prevent unhealthy brain programming. This may be the most important workbook in years. After 10 years of iPhones and Androids, we may actually have less freedom in this digital world. The message contained within the "Digital Vortex Survival Guide" will stir you and shake you. Hopefully it will also move parents and families to find true freedom in moderation and authenticity within this digital world. – **Daniel J van Ingen, Psy.D., Clinical Psychologist, Parenting Doctors, Author of "You Are Your child's Best Psychologist: 7 Keys to Parenting with Excellence."**

Our youth is our future, and we all must be concerned with the growing numbers of youth addicted to video games and other social and entertainment media. Their brains are exposed to these harmful contents at a time they are developing, forever changing neuronal connections. With excessive exposure to addictive media, the brains on one hand develop neuronal connections of unhealthy habits and thoughts, and on the other hand are held back from developing healthy neuronal connections needed for a happy life. In this carefully designed book, Julie Doan, R.N., and Christie Walsh provide, in a step by step approach, education to understand what happens to our brains and what our brains need, and the spiritual and behavioral tools to arrive there. By doing so, this book becomes an invaluable tool in educating our youth and providing them with a life of purpose, a Godly life. – **K. Drorit Gaines, Ph.D. Clinical and Forensic Neuropsychologist UCLA Department of Pediatrics, Faculty.**

"Digital Vortex Survival Guide" – a new workbook written by Julie Doan and Christie Walsh provides an interesting point of view for the potential threats of new technology overuse. As research data show, in 2016, 24% of children below the age of 10 regularly (on a daily basis) were using the internet without parental control and among teenagers, it was 98%. Screens and digital media are a huge part of everyday life for adults and kids. This digital revolution sneaked into our lives almost unnoticed and we were never taught how to use tech in a way which is safe for our family relations and for the development of kids. The authors present a Christian perspective on this new challenge and a great synthesis of scientific knowledge on learning, brain functioning and development and addictive behaviors. Moreover, the workbook offers a set of questions and advice on how to deal with daily challenges in a healthy way, preventing from escaping into new technology overuse. Personally, I found it interesting and inspiring and I think it will be an interesting proposition for many families sharing Christian values. – **Mateusz Gola, Ph.D., Assistant Professor of Psychology, Head of Clinical Neuroscience Lab at Institute of Psychology, Polish Academy of Sciences. The author of several scientific publications on psychological and neural mechanisms of problematic pornography use.**

We have to get our heads out of the sand to get our kids' heads out of their devices. Here Julie Doan and Christie Walsh take us through a process to help us lead our children (and our students and ourselves) to use these devices to enhance and not control our lives. I have known Julie for many years and have followed her with "Hooked on Games" and Real Battle ministries and have become an unabashed fan. Julie and Christie are experts in the tricky area of digital media and maybe just as important are realistic, compassionate, and empathetic in their approach to this burgeoning problem. I hope you will work through this workbook and take control of these electronic devices which are clearly the opium of our times. - **Thomas A Oetting, M.S., M.D., Rudy And Margaret Perez Professor of Ophthalmology, University of Iowa.**

The "Digital Vortex Survival Guide" is a welcome resource to address the urgent problem of overexposure to digital media. Authors Julie Doan and Christie Walsh offer valuable medical and psychological perceptions integrated with the timeless and practical wisdom of the Bible. Today's parents and youth will find a pathway through the dangerous digital maze by reading and interacting with this helpful workbook. – **Dr. Jerry Rueb, Lead Pastor, Author, Educator, World Missions Advocate, Cornerstone Church, Long Beach, CA.**

The great strength of this book is that it has just the right mix of scripture, science, and thought provoking questions to help most any teen make good choices when it comes to technology. I highly recommend this book! - **John D. Foubert, Ph.D., Author, "How Pornography Harms", Endowed Professor, Oklahoma State University**

This outstanding resource is needed now more than ever in our society, a perfect blend of scientific facts and research with timeless eternal truths that can free and protect young person to old person from the barrage and pull of excessive digital media tsunami that we must all learn to surf on and not be destroyed in. I have personally used this survival Guide and it has been a huge help for myself and my family, both when I'm here in the USA, or the Battle fields of Iraq. - **Victor Marx, Evangelist, Chairman of the Board and President Victor Marx Ministries.**

What would God say about technology? In the "Digital Vortex Survival Guide", Doan and Walsh creatively weave religion with media science and research, offering thought provoking questions which guide readers toward improved technology knowledge and management. If you want to align your family's use of technology with God's plan for health and well being, you must experience the journey toward family exploration and reconnection through this wonderful workbook. – **Cris Rowan, author of "Virtual Child – The terrifying truth about what technology is doing to children."**

If you worry about the minds of children in the digital era, then you have to read this groundbreaking book to understand how to integrate digital media into young lives without harming development. Julie Doan and Christie Walsh combine deep Christian values with easy to understand neuroscience in a book and program that will help adults to empower youth as they grow in a digital reality, unlike anything that's ever existed in human history. - **Wayne Elsey, Father, Granddad, Founder of Soles4Souls, Head Coach - Elsey Enterprises.**

I believe it to be both crucial and critical that while living in this specific hour of human history that we truly possess a clear understanding of Revelation not just Information. Amidst the exterior confusion, darkness and mass distraction of the age, a NEW MIND-SKIN for the NEW-WINE SKIN is required. Here in this extensive and interactive workbook, Julie Doan and Christie Walsh expose and grant us access into this most fascinating subject of the brain and its scientific neurological behaviors. Exposing and unlocking us into the real effects regarding the prevalent digital & social media world we're all surrounded by. The balance of both the scientific and Biblical scriptural insight of TRUTH contained here within these pages is to be compared to that like a treasure chest of Gold. Providing, supplying and equipping us all with the necessary tools of engagement into today's world. It's my pleasure and honor to HIGHLY endorse and STRONGLY encourage ALL, parents and families, to resource themselves with this book. - **Matthew Pollock, Lead Pastor The Way Family Church, Murrieta, CA.**

Being a Christian Physician for over 22 years, I am surprised to find that I have learned so much from this book. Julie Doan and Christie Walsh really made it clear in regard to the Biblical teachings of the Bible, the negative effects of gaming in regards to the cognitive function and the disorders that follow. It has moved me to take gaming and its effects more seriously and helped me recognize these effects in my younger family. I would recommend this book to not only clinicians, but parents and Christians alike. It is a good read for the mind and soul. - **Anthony Phan, M.D.**

As a mother of a child, who committed suicide after becoming addicted to video games, I find the "Digital Vortex Survival Guide" as an in-depth workbook, which educates teens from a Christian and medical prospective, how overuse of digital media can affect the brain and steal their lives (physical, mental, spiritual and emotional). Also, it allows the students to create a reference, as to why and how they can apply this knowledge today, to make "wiser" choices with the gift of life, that God has given each of us. - **Liz Woolley, Founder of On-Line Gamers Anonymous.**

Julie Doan and Christie Walsh have developed a practical, step-by-step guide to help youth understand the impact of screen technology on their developing minds and hearts. They offer the basics of brain science to provide an overview of the developing brain. This, coupled with questions for self-reflection, provides a framework for choosing how to support one's own development in a productive way. Studying this workbook can give youth guidance in developing their God-given potential and, with that, a fuller, more creative life. - **Gloria DeGaetano, founder and director, Parent Coaching Institute; author, "Parenting Well in Our Media Age: Keeping Our Kids Human."**

Julie Doan and Christie Walsh, in their workbook the "Digital Vortex Survival Guide", clearly lay out the path by which children, young adults and adults are unsuspectingly enticed into the digital vortex, why it's a dangerous place to be, and chapter by chapter, how to extract oneself and one's family from harm. Through the identification and connection to God's Plan, Julie and Christie lay out a path to follow to decrease the negative impact of media and increase the positive impact of connection to God. This workbook will equip children, teens and families with the knowledge needed and actions to take to increase connection to God, resilience, and healthy, productive life. This workbook would benefit any family who regularly uses digital media, and if followed, is truly an escape guide from the digital vortex. - **Cynthia Reed, R.N., Ph.D., Executive Director, Iowa Lions Eye Bank.**

Julie Doan and Christie Walsh's "Digital Vortex Survival Guide" is a must-read for all who want to understand how to survive in this new era of digital media. As a recovering video game addict of ten years, I know all too well the negative impact digital media and video games can have on your life, as they caused me to drop out of high school, deceive my family, and even write a suicide note. Today, we live in a world where digital media is integrated into our lives, and it's not going anywhere. To live our purpose and realize our fullest potential, we must learn how to navigate this new world. That is why I strongly recommend the "Digital Vortex Survival Guide" to those seeking to not only understand the problem, but to learn practical solutions to recover that work. - **Cam Adair, Founder of Game Quitters, Recovering Video Game Addict of 10 Years.**

Foreword

We are living in some of the most unique times in all of history. This is the first generation of people that GOD has allowed to come together and unite since the Tower of Babel. Technology is not good or bad. Technology allows your child to connect to the entire world, and the entire world (including the evil and bad guys) can connect to your child. At any one time, there are over 1 million predators online hunting for victims.

I believe GOD will hold us responsible for how we parent and lead this generation. Technology can be used to grow us as individuals and honor and glorify GOD or it can be used to develop levels of evil never before understood by man. The Internet can be the great equalizer. Today, the poorest child can access the same educational materials that a student at Harvard University will be exposed to. However, it also means that child can access pornographic and violent video games. Children can spend their days enslaved to gaining acceptance and approval of total strangers, competing for allusive approval through chat rooms and live streaming of interactive pornography and video games.

GOD has entrusted us as parents and leaders to educate our teens to use technology for the glory of GOD and to resist evil. This workbook prepared by Julie Doan and Christie Walsh is truly cutting edge ministry. Having worked with Andrew Doan, M.D., Ph.D. and his wife Julie, I highly endorse this work. It is extremely critical for our youth to understand the impact of technology on their physical and emotional development and make informed and educated decisions so they can develop into the Christian leadership of tomorrow.

I believe GOD has called on all Christian leadership to step back and understand the impact technology has on our youth. This is the first generation to be given this much access, and GOD will hold us responsible for laying the foundation that will influence our youth for generations to come.

Congratulations Julie and Christie, you have done an extraordinary service to parents and teachers around the world. This is one of the most important works available to our society. It is my prayer that Christians around the globe will embrace and utilize this workbook to educate our leaders and our young people. It is by far, the best resource available on the subject.

Opal Singleton

President and CEO, Million Kids (www.MillionKids.org), author of "Seduced"

Introduction

The digital world is designed to grab our attention through the allure of increased productivity, interactivity, and entertainment, all within instant reach of our smartphones and mobile devices. We have endless access to movies, social interactivity, music, games, and anything the human mind creates in a digital environment. This is different than television in the 1970s or 1980s when we had to wait a week or longer for new episodes of our favorite shows. Currently, there is enough digital media, social media, and gaming content to keep a child entertained from birth to 18 years of age, daily around the clock. With moderate digital media use and prosocial focus, our lives have improved, we benefit emotionally, and we can make a positive impact in our communities. Because digital media is created to captivate us and entice us, the brain and body are aroused, similar to consuming a piece of chocolate that stimulates the brain with some dopamine. When digital devices are placed in the hands of young children who have yet to develop self-control, we are observing problems with behaviors, school performance, lack of interest in reading, diminished creativity, temper tantrums, and undesired behaviors. It seems that our mind is constantly searching for ways to increase our time on social media, streaming video, and video games. Clearly, digital media can be incredibly enticing. For most, digital media will just waste time at the expense of other opportunities. For some, digital media is like an addiction, resulting in serious emotional and health problems.

This workbook is designed to explain complex neuroscience with Biblical truths so that teenagers and parents can understand why excessive behaviors and overuse of digital media can affect the brain and will harm brain development. This program is designed to educate, to increase awareness, and to protect you from being sucked into the digital vortex. Some digital media use may be beneficial to our brains and lives; however, excessive use of anything will be harmful. Even water, something that we need adequate amounts of to maintain life, can be toxic to the brain if it is ingested excessively. With water toxicity, the brain swells which may result in seizures and even death. This workbook introduces neuroscience concepts about the brain's reward pathway and explains how and why we seek more time using digital media (e.g. cell phones, streaming movies, video games, social media, and pornography). Too much of our attention and time gets sucked into this digital vortex causing us to not spend time developing the skills that will help us achieve our full potential. Excessive use of digital media is harmful to our brains and health.

Research has shown that we retain about:
- 10% of what we hear,
- 25% of what we hear and read,
- 50% of what we hear, read, and study,
- 75% of what we hear, read, study, and memorize,
- 100% of what we hear, read, study, memorize, and meditate on. (www.navigators.org)

This workbook is designed to be used at Bible camps, summer retreats and for home study. The Bible passages provided are from the King James Version (KJV) or the New King James Version (NKJV). If your church leadership uses a different Bible translation, then please use the translation you feel is most appropriate. While wording may be different in these various translations, we have found that all the translations are consistent with the workbook's application. The most important thing is to pray for the Holy Spirit to give understanding and wisdom pertaining to the Bible passages.

At camps, trained counselors will teach the lessons with demonstrations and presentations. For those working through this book at home, we recommend you watch our videos on www.realbattle.org/digital-vortex/, and then work through the workbook. Each participant should have their own workbook to spend time reading, studying, and memorizing the concepts through self-study, answering questions, and journaling. Color pencils are recommended to have the reader color the line drawings while meditating on what they have heard, read, studied, and memorized. In the back of this workbook, a glossary with a definition of complex terms is provided for reference (terms in the glossary are **bolded** in this workbook). We have also provided space for journaling to improve learning and self-reflection. Together, these activities are proven methodologies to improve learning and creating self-awareness. This book is intended to be used as an introduction to behaviors, digital media, and how our brains are affected by what we do, think, see, hear, and experience. Our goal is to equip teens and families with knowledge so that they can thrive in the digital age and escape being sucked into a digital vortex.

It is in the spirit of empowerment, not judgement, that we have deliberately avoided the term "addiction" in this workbook because few people actually meet the clinical criteria of addiction. Clinical "addiction" reflects dysfunction in five to six areas of a person's life, such as: financial problems, relationship difficulties, withdrawal symptoms, cravings, using to escape negative feelings, continued use even though aware of negative consequences, lying about use, unable to quit, not having enjoyment from other activities, and failure in work or school. A person who has dysfunction in one or two areas listed will not qualify to receive the diagnosis of addiction. Yet, dysfunction in just one or two areas listed, which is more common, may result in emotional problems, reduce resilience, and cause considerable stress to individuals and their families. Therefore, most people reading this workbook would not be considered clinically addicted. On the other hand, full-blown clinical addiction is not necessary for emotional problems, undesired behaviors, lack of productivity, and sleep deprivation to be associated with excessive use of digital media.

We pray that we have communicated in a forthright yet non-offensive way that enables you to assess what is healthy for you so that you have the time to attain all the skills GOD has blessed you with and to enjoy the people who are in your lives. For more information about our ministry or for educational resources about digital media, **please visit our website: www.realbattle.org**. May the LORD bless you with protection, favor, and wisdom!

Lesson 1

GOD is Real

At that time Jesus answered and said, "I thank You, Father, Lord of heaven and earth, that You have hidden these things from the wise and prudent and have revealed them to babes. Even so, Father, for so it seemed good in Your sight. All things have been delivered to Me by My Father, and no one knows the Son except the Father. Nor does anyone know the Father except the Son, and the one to whom the Son wills to reveal Him. Come to Me, all you who labor and are heavy laden, and I will give you rest. Take My yoke upon you and learn from Me, for I am gentle and lowly in heart, and you will find rest for your souls. For My yoke is easy and My burden is light."

- Matthew 11:25-30, NKJV

For those using this book at home, we recommend watching the videos on:
www.realbattle.org/digital-vortex/, and then work through this lesson.

Everything in nature, in our world, and in our universe, points to the existence of GOD. From the Bible, we understand that GOD is triune, meaning that GOD exists as three distinct entities, yet all three are one. We see this concept of three in one and one in three with **the periodic table of elements**. Every **element, mineral,** and **chemical compound** exists as three states of matter given the proper physical conditions. Even **molecules**, like H_2O or water, exist as three distinct physical forms at certain temperatures, pressures, and conditions. Water can be a solid (ice), liquid, or gas (steam). Moreover, ice, fluid, and steam molecules are all water, but ice is not fluid nor steam.

> *"Everything in nature, in our world, and in our universe, points to the existence of GOD."*

Drawing from the above example, GOD reveals Himself to us as the Father, the Son, and the Holy Spirit (see Figure 1). We know GOD is real when the Son, Jesus Christ, walked the Earth, performed miracles, died, and rose from the dead. The moment Jesus revealed Himself and rose from the dead, we are certain GOD is real. Today, GOD continues to show Himself to people who seek Him. In Matthew 11, Jesus encourages us to lean on Him by being yoked with Him. When we have problems, struggles, and hardships, we can lean on GOD. Jesus uses the analogy of being yoked to Him. Yokes are used on teams of two oxen to pull a plow. Similarly, when we ask, we can be yoked with Jesus, the Son of GOD and the Creator of all. Jesus will give us rest, give us life, and assist us with bearing the weight of our burdens.

All of us struggle with difficulties in life. We all have hardships. With GOD, we face life with confidence, understanding, and peace. Before you embark on these lessons, pray to GOD for His wisdom.

Pray this:

Dear LORD, please help me. Fill me with your Holy Spirit and give me understanding, wisdom, and courage. Teach me how to apply what I learn at camp, from my leaders, and from my lessons to live life with wisdom, so that I may serve you better. In Jesus' name I pray, amen!

Figure 1: GOD is Triune. The relationship of the Father, the Son, and the Holy Spirit to GOD.

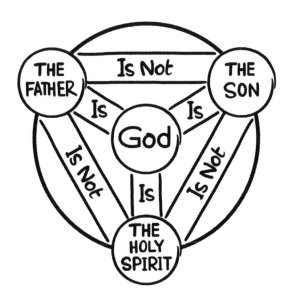

Figure 2: GOD Shares Our Burdens. When troubled or burdened, Jesus will help us and be yoked with us if invited.

Points to consider and discuss:

1) What circumstances have you experienced or observed that provide evidence for the existence of GOD?

_____

_____

_____

_____

_____

2) Why should you trust that GOD is interested in what is best for you?

_____

_____

_____

_____

_____

3) How has GOD helped you in your life?

_____

_____

_____

_____

_____

4) Improve this lesson by filling out the survey questions on page 73.

Lesson 2

Brain Development in a Nutshell

For You formed my inward parts; You covered me in my mother's womb. I will praise You, for I am fearfully and wonderfully made; Marvelous are Your works, And that my soul knows very well.

- Psalm 139: 13-14, NKJV

For those using this book at home, we recommend watching the videos on: www.realbattle.org/digital-vortex/, and then work through this lesson.

The human brain matures from the back of the brain to the front of the brain as we age (see Figure 3). As the brain matures, **neuronal connections** that are used often are strengthened. Hence, **neurons** that fire together, wire together. On the other hand, using the brain for learning negative skills or experiencing negative experiences encourages unwanted connections. Our brains have about 100 billion neurons. Neurons do not replicate like other cells. Neurons are cells that connect to other neurons and enable different areas of the brain to communicate and to control the body. These neuronal connections make up pathways controlling feelings, thoughts, memories, senses, and physical movements. Because of neurons and their connections, the brain becomes the control center that makes us who we are and allows us to think, move, and interact with others. The front of the brain consists of areas that control higher reasoning, emotional maturity, and self-control, also known as higher executive functions. Neuronal connections that are not used often are removed or pruned away as the brain matures because the brain realizes that if a person has not used these connections, they must not be necessary. Because the brain is extremely efficient and is confined to a limited space inside our skull, it goes through a process called pruning (just like in gardening). The front of the brain controlling higher executive functions begins the pruning process during the early teenage years with complete maturation by around age 25. Experience as we age gives us wisdom. Therefore, as we age, we make wiser decisions and understand more complex concepts because our brains are older with reinforced connections and less used connections removed. Neuronal pruning is the very essence of the saying "use it or lose it!"

"It takes 10,000 hours to develop expertise."

During the pruning process, it is very important to practice and develop healthy behaviors and to avoid harmful behaviors. Medical researchers have estimated that our skills and talents are determined: 1) by our **DNA** and 2) by how much time is devoted to developing our skills and talents through repetition and practice. It appears that about one-third of how well we do something is programmed by the **genes** in our DNA. Two-thirds of how well we do something is determined by how much time we devote to practicing and developing the skill. In the book *"Outliers: The Story of Success"*, Malcom Gladwell stated that it takes 10,000 hours to develop expertise. Let's consider a person with the **innate** ability to play football better than the average person. If that person does not practice and develop skills related to football, then as the brain prunes and removes connections that are not used, this person will not develop **expertise** in football skills. On the other hand, if the same person devotes 10,000 hours in developing football skills, then the brain reinforces the connections associated with these skills and the person will become an expert. 10,000 hours of practice is 40 hours a week for 5 years, 20 hours a week for 10 years, or 10 hours a week for 20 years. The less time we devote per week to practicing our skills, the longer it will take to master these skills. Because of brain pruning, it is best to practice those things we desire to become when our brains are young and easily programmed.

What we see, hear, feel, think, and experience can seriously affect our brains when they are not fully mature, or pruned. A brain that is young is more programmable (greater plasticity), and therefore young children may harm their brains if exposed to any behavior in excess, such as too much time with bullying, using drugs, and playing with digital media. Also, **trauma** and bad experiences in our youth affect us in adulthood and may be vivid in our memories. We should protect our brains from bad thoughts, hurtful feelings, and harmful behaviors. Although we grow with challenges and hardships, a young brain should be protected from excessive and abusive thoughts and behaviors. When our brains mature, we are better equipped to tackle trials and tribulations.

Young brains are particularly **vulnerable** to risky and addictive behaviors. Because the front of the brain does not fully mature until age 25, we do not have the reasoning abilities to make wise decisions. Therefore, we make more mistakes and make poor decisions in our youth. If we apply this knowledge to create guidelines for technology usage at each age, we can better ensure that the vulnerable mind of a child does not get damaged by overusing digital media technology. While young, it is best to seek guidance and direction from people (parents and experts) who have more experience and wisdom to understand the long-term consequences of destructive behaviors. It is also best to seek knowledge and wisdom from the Bible. GOD's wisdom in the Bible is eternal.

Figure 3: Brain Pruning and Functions of the Brain. These are images of brain scans taken from

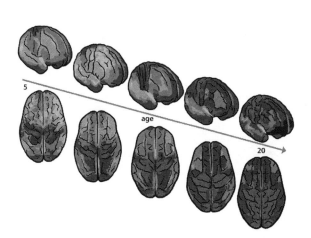

people at different ages. Lighter shades represent areas of the brain that have not been pruned. Darker shades represent brain tissue that has been pruned where less used neuronal connections have been removed. The front of the brain controls higher executive functions, which does not mature fully until age 25. Recreated utilizing data from Paul Thompson, Ph.D. UCLA Laboratory of Neuroimaging. The image below shows areas in the brain that control various functions.

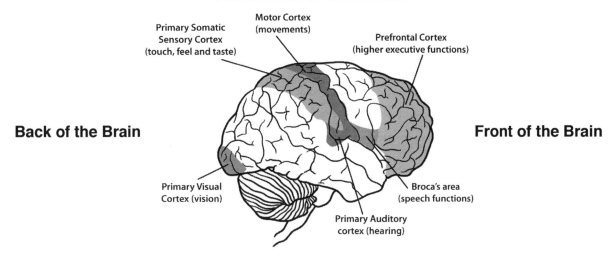

Functions of the Brain

Primary Somatic Sensory Cortex (touch, feel and taste)

Motor Cortex (movements)

Prefrontal Cortex (higher executive functions)

Back of the Brain

Front of the Brain

Primary Visual Cortex (vision)

Broca's area (speech functions)

Primary Auditory cortex (hearing)

Points to consider and discuss:

1) Share an early childhood situation that had a negative impact on your life. Share an early childhood situation that had a positive impact on your life.

_____

_____

_____

_____

_____

2) Can old memories stimulate your brain and body to become aroused? Give an example.

_____

_____

_____

_____

_____

3) Although we all need both positive and negative experiences to shape who we are today, why is it important to protect our young and developing minds from unnecessary trauma, negativity, and addictive behaviors?

_____

_____

_____

_____

_____

4) Improve this lesson by filling out the survey questions on page 73.

Lesson 3

Stay Sober and Alert

And do not be **drunk** with wine, in which is dissipation; but be filled with the Spirit, speaking to one another in psalms and hymns and spiritual songs, singing and making melody in your heart to the Lord, giving thanks always for all things to God the Father in the name of our Lord Jesus Christ, submitting to one another in the fear of God.

- Ephesians 5:18-21, NKJV

For those using this book at home, we recommend watching the videos on:
www.realbattle.org/digital-vortex/, and then work through this lesson.

In Lesson 2, we learned about neurons and how they form pathways in the brain to send messages that enable our body to perform all of its functions. Lesson 3 is about the **neurotransmitters** in the brain and how they make us feel. A neurotransmitter is a chemical that sends messages from one neuron to another. Every second of every day, billions of brain cells transmit signals to each other by sending neurotransmitters through their connections called synapses. These neuronal connections control everything we feel and do, including learning, memorizing, planning, reasoning, and enabling movement. Learning how neurons and neurotransmitters control the body has enabled science to develop medications that interact at the molecular level and can be used to help the body deal with different undesirable physical sensations, such as pain. The neurotransmitter called dopamine plays a major role in behaviors that are motivated by rewards and makes us feel good. When we do something that achieves a reward, our brain dopamine levels increase so we feel pleasure. Addictive drugs and behaviors increase dopamine levels in the brain and when overused, cause physical and emotional harm to the body and mind.

When we **ingest** a medication or a drug, the pharmaceutical molecule binds to **receptors** in the body and brain to initiate **physiological** changes in the body. Let's look at the **molecular action** of cocaine. **Cocaine** is used medically as a painkiller, or anesthetic. However, some people abuse cocaine as a way to escape life. Cocaine acts first on the brain by blocking the recycling mechanism of **dopamine**, a **neurotransmitter** in the brain. Because the recycling mechanism is blocked, dopamine levels in the brain rise and **stimulate neuronal pathways** in the brain's reward pathways, causing the euphoric feeling. Dopamine also stimulates the **hypothalamus** to activate the **pituitary gland** to release **hormones**. These pituitary hormones will stimulate other glands in the body, such as the adrenal glands, to arouse the body. The activation of **the hypothalamus-pituitary-adrenal pathway** is associated with the fight or flight response. We tend to fight for things that make us feel good or to protect our self-interests. We will run away from situations that make us feel anxious or bad. The hormones associated with the fight or flight response prepare our bodies to deal with stressful situations. Keep in mind that stress can be both good and bad. Going on vacations and having fun makes us feel good but also places stress on our bodies. This is an example of good stress. Getting into arguments with our families stresses our bodies and minds, and these situations make us feel anxious, fearful, angry, and stressed. This is an example of bad stress. In general, we should engage in activities that are positive stressors, and we should avoid situations that are negative stressors. Drugs and behaviors activate similar neurochemistry.

> *"When we do anything excessively, our minds are not sober..."*

In Ephesians 5, we are encouraged to seek stress relief and arousal by being filled with the Holy Spirit. The LORD will fill us up with feel good stimulation of brain reward pathways and with feel good hormones in our blood stream through the hypothalamus-pituitary-adrenal axis and other hormonal pathways. GOD also created things in this world to give us pleasure and to assist us in stress relief. The activities listed in Ephesians 5, listening to music, singing and being thankful are all activities and behaviors that make us feel good from the hormones that are stimulated when we do them. In our society, we have social media, video games, and an abundance of entertainment to help us feel good and help us in our lives. Digital media increase brain dopamine and release of hormones. However, we must not overuse nor be **drunk** in these activities. Moderation in activities is important to our emotional and physical health.

Moderation and rest are important because as we stimulate our brains and body, the brain and body reduce the levels of hormones released when exposed to the same drug or behavior. The reward pathways also respond less. This is known as **tolerance**. As we do something excessively, we must do more of it to feel stimulated. With drugs, this means higher dosage of the drug is required to feel the same relief from pain or sensation caused by the drug. With behaviors, this means more time devoted to the activity and more arousing stimuli. When we do anything excessively, our minds are not sober, we are less likely to hear GOD's Word, and we are less likely to make wise decisions.

Here is how we can apply moderation to digital media. If we use social media 30 minutes a day to help us relax and communicate with friends, we feel happy and recharged. It gives our minds a break from the long school or work day and recharges us to start our homework, sports practice, or chores. However, if that 30 minutes becomes 3 hours, we have just created stress in our life. There is not enough time to do a good job on the tasks that we need to complete. We may get less sleep because we need to finish our work. In addition, the additional time spent on digital media has most likely over stimulated our brains with all the **"feel good" hormones** so, we cannot focus. It is as if we are drunk on our own neurochemistry and hormones! So, this is why we need to understand our limitations. Realize that if we lose track of time while looking at our phones, social media or video games that we should set a timer or ask someone to let us know it is time to stop. You can figure out a solution that works for your routine.

Figure 4: Hypothalamus-Pituitary-Adrenal Pathway. Sight, smells, tastes, touch, and sounds activate the reward pathways in the brain, stimulating the hypothalamus to send signals to the pituitary gland. The pituitary gland is located at the bottom of the brain. The pituitary controls hormonal release into the blood stream by activating glands in the body, such as the adrenal glands, thyroid, and **gonads**.

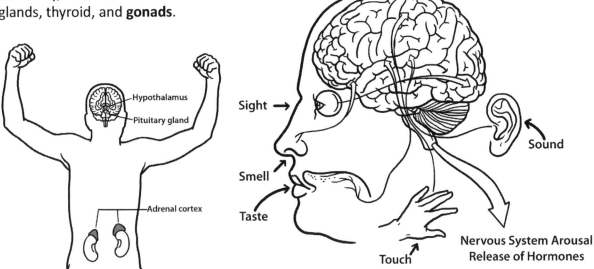

Points to consider and discuss:

1) What behaviors do you use to help deal with stress and escape from life?

_____

_____

_____

_____

_____

2) What problems do you encounter when behaviors are excessive and become all-consuming in your daily life?

_____

_____

_____

_____

_____

3) Discuss types of digital media that stimulate arousal and emotions.

_____

_____

_____

_____

4) Improve this lesson by filling out the survey questions on page 73.

Lesson 4

Monkey See, Monkey Do

"The lamp of the body is the eye. If, therefore, your eye is good, your whole body will be full of light. But if your eye is bad, your whole body will be full of darkness. If, therefore, the light that is in you is darkness, how great is that darkness!"

- Matthew 6:22-23, NKJV

I will set nothing wicked before my eyes: I hate the work of those who fall away; It shall not cling to me.

-Psalm 101:3 NKJV

For those using this book at home, we recommend watching the videos on:
www.realbattle.org/digital-vortex/, and then work through this lesson.

In lesson 3, we described how molecular pharmaceuticals, such as cocaine, interact with **receptors** in the brain and body to **arouse** our bodies. Similarly, things we look at will also affect our bodies. In Matthew 6, Jesus said that the lamp of the body is the eye. If we fill our sight with good things, then our whole body will be filled with light. If we fill our sight with bad things, then our whole body will be full of darkness. Things we look at affect the body through patterns of **light photons** hitting our **photoreceptors** in our eyes (see Figure 5). Photons of light hit the photoreceptors in the retina of the eye to stimulate activation of neuronal pathways that originate from the nerve layers in our eyes, travel through the optic nerves to our brain, and stimulate the brain. Brain stimulation can also activate brain reward pathways and the hypothalamus-pituitary-adrenal and other hormonal pathways. Depending on what we look at, brain and hormonal activation will influence how we feel, such as: anger, fear, sadness, empathy, joy, pleasure, lust, and many other feelings. As we expose ourselves to excessive amounts of sensory **stimuli** (sight, sound, taste, smell, and touch), the brain and hormonal pathways develop tolerance. With excessive visual images and videos, we seek more arousing visual stimuli and more deviant visual stimuli when we develop tolerance. Hearing, smell, taste, and touch will send information to the brain and activate hormonal systems like the visual system.

> *"We must be careful about what we expose our mind and body to with our eyes, ears, and sensory organs."*

The sensory organs act on the mind and body to arouse us, similar to drugs. We must be careful about what we expose our mind and body to with our eyes, ears, and sensory organs. Video games, social media, and pornography are visual, auditory, and tactile stimuli that arouse the mind and body. These activities change the way we think and change our bodies' hormones. Some of these activities, such as prosocial video games, educational video games, and social media, can have positive benefits on our minds, bodies, and emotional health. For instance, using social media to stay connected to family and friends has incredible benefit. However, when used excessively, we will develop **tolerance**, and we will devote excessive time and seek more arousing activities through digital media to feel stimulated. Even with video games and social media, moderation and rest are important. All digital activities (video games, social media, watching videos, and using cell phones) should not consume more than 1 to 2 hours a day. People who use more than 3 hours of digital media per day for entertainment can develop emotional and behavioral problems.

Dr. Victoria Dunckley explains the Electronic Screen Syndrome in her book, "*Reset your Child's Brain*" pages 35-39. She explains that the unnaturally bright light from the screen of a digital device is transmitted by the optic nerve which communicates a signal to the pineal gland that it is daylight. So, the pineal gland does not produce melatonin for sleep because it does not realize that it is night time due to the optic nerve responding to the bright light of the screen. If a person is staring at a bright screen in bed, they may disrupt their body clock's sleep cycle. In addition, the stimulation caused from the quick movements of the images and the bright colors adds to sensory overload that will stimulate more neurotransmitters and hormones, making sleep difficult. It is well known that sleep deprivation leads to behavioral, emotional, and mental problems. With prolonged sleep deprivation and dysregulation of the hypothalamus-pituitary-adrenal pathway, mental disorders like depression, anxiety, bipolar disorder, and psychotic disorders may develop. Dr. Dunckley has discovered that unplugging from digital screens for 30 days can reduce and even resolve behavioral problems, poor grades, ADHD, and mental disorders (either misdiagnosed or atypical presentation due to electronic screen syndrome).

As we unplug from digital devices, the first week may be associated with anxiety, depression, anger, and emotional fluctuations. This is natural as we reset our brains and hormonal levels. Time is required for the brain and body to establish a new **baseline** of arousal. As time goes on, these negative feelings subside, we think clearer, and we feel stronger. We do not have to be clinically addicted to experience negative feelings during the **tech-free period**. Healthy people can feel these emotions when unplugging from digital devices. Non-addicted people can also feel these emotions when unplugging from digital devices because their brains are adjusting to being tech free. If you are feeling increasingly depressed and anxious, please tell your adult leader or an adult you trust so they can get you help.

Figure 5: Light and the Optic Nerve. On the left side of the diagram, photons of light travel through the eye and hit the photoreceptors in the retina at the back of the eye. The retinal photoreceptors stimulate the nerve fibers to fire and transmit signals to the brain via the optic nerve.

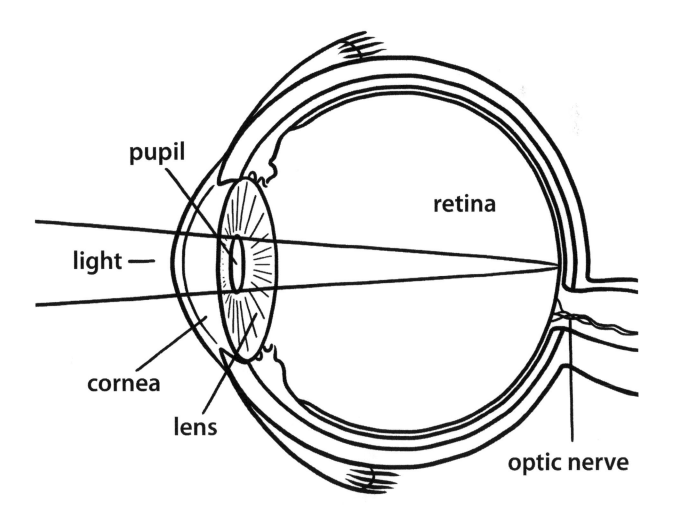

Points to consider and discuss:

1) Are movies more arousing with or without sound and music? Can music stimulate your brain and body like a stimulating drug?

_____

_____

_____

_____

_____

2) Do you use digital media to help escape from life and from problems?

_____

_____

_____

_____

_____

3) When we overuse digital media, what problems do we encounter with relationships, with school work, and with GOD's plans?

_____

_____

_____

_____

_____

4) Improve this lesson by filling out the survey questions on page 73.

Lesson 5

Motivated by Rewards

Seek good and not evil, That you may live; So the Lord God of hosts will be with you, As you have spoken.

– Amos 5: 14, NKJV

And do not be conformed to this world, but be transformed by the renewing of your mind, that you may prove what is that good and acceptable and perfect will of God.

- Romans: 12:2, NKJV

For those using this book at home, we recommend watching the videos on: www.realbattle.org/digital-vortex/, and then work through this lesson.

The **reward pathways** in our brains motivate our behavior. We tend to seek things that are pleasurable, enjoyable, fun, and self-benefiting. Without our reward pathways, we would not receive the arousal and hormones necessary for us to seek food, shelter, and life. GOD created us with reward pathways so that we live, seek purpose, and thrive on the Earth.

Problems develop when we abuse the reward pathways to escape our troubles by using **addictive** behaviors. We also create problems when we seek rewards associated with sinful behaviors. Usually, rewards associated with evil and sin give short-term, immediate gains at the expense of long-term accomplishments. On the other hand, rewards associated with good usually provide long-term, delayed gains. Seeking good behaviors requires self-discipline, sacrifice, and patience, which are **higher executive functions** that develop as we get older and with practice. As we practice self-discipline, sacrifice, and patience, our brains strengthen the memories and **neuronal pathways** associated with these desired behaviors. Therefore, with thoughts, we can physically change our brains and our behavior as is promised to us in Romans 12:2, NKJV: "And do not be conformed to this world, but be transformed by the renewing of your mind, that you may prove what is that good and acceptable and perfect will of God."

Seeking rewards is neither good nor bad. We are wired to be motivated by rewards. We must practice seeking rewards that are associated with good and avoid rewards associated with sin. In the digital age, we are surrounded by the potential for constant rewards such as Facebook likes or scoring points in our favorite games. Stimulating the hormones that make us feel good associated with excessive use of digital media can lead to problems when we sacrifice time with people, for sleep, and for important tasks. We live during a time when it is possible for children to interact with digital screens all day and night. In 2010, the Kaiser Foundation estimated that the average American child uses digital screens for entertainment 7 hours 38 minutes daily.

> *"We practice who we want to become, and we must be careful what we practice and how we program our brains."*

As we age, we practice who we want to become, and we must be careful what we practice and how we program our brains. When we spend too much time with digital media, there can be significant problems due to the brain's inability to distinguish reality from virtual fantasy. We produce the same hormones for fear, excitement and pleasure from the video games as if we were doing the activity. So, a person who focuses only on virtual stimulations for feel good hormones will not develop the higher executive functions necessary to generate the same amount of pleasure from real world activities that require more effort than the twitch of a finger.

We propose an analogy to clarify how our nervous system may develop when exposed to excessive time engaging in gaming, social media, or other digital media activities (as described by Dr. Andrew Doan and team, Yale J Biol Med. 2015 Sep 3;88(3):319-24). Observe your left hand. The thumb will represent the brain areas associated with all the benefits of digital media: quick analytical skills, improved hand-eye-coordination, and perhaps improved reflexes. The index finger will represent the brain areas associated with communication skills. The middle finger will represent behaviors associated with social bonding with family and friends. The ring finger will represent the capacity to recognize emotions of both self and others (empathy). Lastly, the little finger will represent the brain areas associated with self-control. These higher executive functions are all learned behaviors, requiring time and practice before we master them well enough to stimulate pleasure hormones. When we spend an average of 7h 38m in front of a digital screen for entertainment, we exceed seven-fold the recommended daily dosage for healthy screen time. There is not enough time left in a day to master the higher executive functions of social bonding, communication, empathy and self-control. Folding the fingers into the palm of your hand represents this situation. As the brain matures, and these areas (or fingers) are not used, the result is an adult who is "all thumbs" in their thinking. They possess quick analytical skills and quick reflexes, but are lacking in communication skills, having few bonds with people, exhibiting little empathy, and showing minimal self-control.

Figure 6: Brain Reward Pathways. We are motivated by reward pathways in the brain associated with seeking things that feel good and avoiding things that feel bad.

Brain Reward Pathways

Run away from things that **feel bad** ⟷ Run to things that **feel good**

Points to consider and discuss:

1) What foods do you eat that make you feel good and are healthy for you?

_____

_____

_____

_____

_____

2) What happens to your body and mood when you continually overeat your favorite foods above?

_____

_____

_____

_____

_____

3) What happens to your attitudes when you overuse digital media? What are the consequences of digital media overuse?

_____

_____

_____

_____

_____

4) Improve this lesson by filling out the survey questions on page 73.

Lesson 6

The Reward Pathway and Fight or Flight Response

A satisfied soul **loathes** the honeycomb, But to a hungry soul every bitter thing is sweet.

– Proverbs 27: 7, NKJV

For those using this book at home, we recommend watching the videos on:
www.realbattle.org/digital-vortex/, and then work through this lesson.

We have considered good and bad behaviors that stimulate dopamine release in the brain reward pathways: eating food, exercising, consuming sugar, taking drugs, listening to music, watching movies, playing video games, engaging with people on social media, and behaviors that give us pleasure. The most stimulating behaviors are those that activate the fight or flight response associated with the **hypothalamus-pituitary-adrenal pathway**. Stimulating and arousing behaviors increase our heart rate, our perspiration, and release of hormones that arouse us to action. **Digital media** stimulates the brain and body similar to the real activity. This is why digital media with sexual content and violence are so potently (powerfully) stimulating, because this content provides thrills and excitement that are primitive and common to all mammals. The virtual stimuli provide hormonal stimulation or reward, with much less effort.

If we are not careful, then our thoughts **gravitate** to things that are sexual and violent. As we engage in behaviors excessively and consume extensive amounts of digital media, our bodies develop **tolerance** which reduces the arousal associated with these activities. In Proverbs 27:7, the Bible teaches that if we over **indulge** in pleasures, then even the sweetness of the honeycomb tastes horrible. Imagine stuffing our faces with sweets and sugar before a nice dinner. The dinner will be less satisfying after over-stimulating our taste buds with sugar. However, with discipline and restraint from excessive stimulation, even things that may be bitter in this world will seem sweet to our senses. When we exhibit self-control, and avoid over-stimulation, we will find life more enjoyable and exciting. For example, we will even miss our annoying sisters or brothers when we are separated from them for weeks at camp.

> *"When we fill our minds with explicit images, real human beings and real relationships appear cumbersome, less exciting, and under-arousing."*

One form of digital media that is destroying our motivation for real relationships is pornography. When we fill our minds with explicit images, real human beings and real relationships appear cumbersome, less exciting, and under-arousing. People who view pornography may even develop physical and emotional **dysfunction** when interacting with people (from Dr. Andrew Doan and team, Behav Sci (Basel). 2016 Aug 5;6(3)). Remember, we practice what we want to become. Our brains equate the virtual relational experiences online with how the mind expects rewards from real human relational experiences. The problem is that real human relationships are rarely as exciting as our virtual relationships because the virtual world is not based on truth. Humans rarely appear as they do in digital media and video games. So, if we seek the same amount of stimulation attained in virtual (fake) relationships online, we will be disappointed because real humans are not super heroes nor super models created by our imaginations. If we put effort into seeking relationships with real people, we will get more pleasure from face-to-face encounters the more we have them. With repetition, our neuronal connections get stronger and it takes less effort to complete the task that gets the reward. Thus, the more often we are around people, the better we get at being around people. We will seek out people to interact with daily and feel more pleasure from it.

Video games when played excessively will destroy personal motivation. Video games are designed to give us the arousal associated with epic challenges, epic fantasies and epic victories, in virtual, fake environments. Real-life accomplishments seem trivial to the epic wins in video games. When utilized more than 30 to 60 minutes daily, video games provide short-term, immediate gains at the expense of long-term, real-life accomplishments. Because we practice who we want to become, by overusing video games, we crave digital fantasies which demotivates us to pursue real-life goals requiring more effort. Eventually, habitual digital media overuse raises the baseline amounts of hormones and neurochemistry required to feel good so that real life cannot produce that level of stimulation. So, the brain prefers the virtual path of fantasy that earns more reward with minimal effort, while becoming bored with real life.

The reward pathway is the brain's way of telling our body that an experience was good and that we want to do it again. Stimuli such as sugar, sex and drugs are some of the most powerful and are associated with dopamine release. The ventral tegmental area (VTA) releases dopamine when a pleasurable stimuli is experienced. The VTA sends the dopamine to the nucleus accumbens and the prefrontal cortex. The nucleus accumbens controls motor functions so that when we feel pleasure from doing something, we can physically do it again. The prefrontal cortex helps us focus our attention and plans skills necessary to do the activity again. Our brain stores the memory so that we can repeat the reward pathway process again when the same stimulus is experienced in the future. Repeating the rewarding experience strengthens neuronal pathways that reinforces the behavior, increasing our tendency to repeat the behavior in the future.

Figure 7: Reward Pathway. The prefrontal cortex, nucleus accumbens, and ventral tegmental area (VTA) control the reward pathway in the brain. Source: National Institute on Drug Abuse

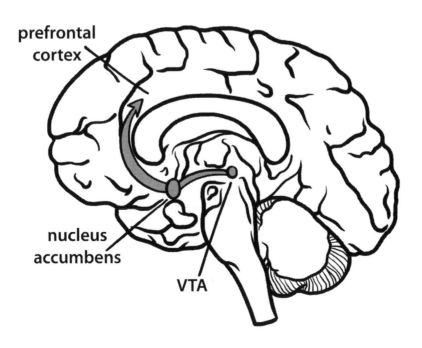

Points to consider and discuss:

1) Which activities on digital screens stimulate and arouse you the most?

_____

_____

_____

_____

_____

2) Have you used digital screens to escape or to deal with stress?

_____

_____

_____

_____

_____

3) Have you struggled with managing your time with digital screens? Why? What can you do to gain control with digital screens?

_____

_____

_____

_____

_____

4) Improve this lesson by filling out the survey questions on page 73.

Lesson 7

The Addiction Pathway

But know this, that in the last days **perilous** times will come: For men will be lovers of themselves, lovers of money, boasters, proud, blasphemers, disobedient to parents, unthankful, unholy, unloving, unforgiving, slanderers, without self-control, brutal, despisers of good, traitors, headstrong, haughty, lovers of pleasure rather than lovers of God, having a form of godliness but denying its power. And from such people turn away! For of this sort are those who creep into households and make captives of gullible women loaded down with sins, led away by various lusts, always learning and never able to come to the knowledge of the truth. Now as Jannes and Jambres resisted Moses, so do these also resist the truth: men of corrupt minds, disapproved concerning the faith; but they will progress no further, for their **folly** will be **manifest** to all, as theirs also was.

– 2 Timothy 3: 1-9, NKJV

For all have sinned and fall short of the glory of God; Being justified freely by his grace through the redemption that is in Christ Jesus.

- Romans 3: 23-24, NKJV

For those using this book at home, we recommend watching the videos on:
www.realbattle.org/digital-vortex/, and then work through this lesson.

The Apostle Paul in 2 Timothy 3, warned of times when people will seek sin and self-pleasure instead of desiring self-control, goodness, and GOD. Some people develop addictive behaviors because of sin. Many people, however, develop addictive behaviors because of poor stress management. In Figure 8, the model for addictive behaviors starts with stress. With poor **stress management**, we crave **rituals** and behaviors to relieve stress. These behaviors may be overeating, drugs, alcohol, anger, arguing, excessive social media, escape with gaming marathons, and overuse of digital media. With overuse, we face the consequences of neglecting relationships, responsibilities, and GOD's plans for us. With consequences, we add to our stress and the entire cycle repeats itself and is reinforced. Because we practice who we become, excessive use of any behavior for stress relief will turn us into addicts.

Addiction does not occur overnight. Addiction develops one day at a time with many poor choices over numerous days. To avoid addiction, we must take our thoughts captive, and we must develop healthy ways to deal with stress. We tend to overuse and abuse things and behaviors that make us feel good and activate the reward pathway during stressful times. Because cauliflower and broccoli do not stimulate the brain and body like sugar, drugs, video games, and pornography, we do not encounter people sitting on the couch popping cauliflower and broccoli to relieve their stress. Therefore, we generally do not see people with cauliflower or broccoli addictions.

"A person struggling with addictive behaviors is really a "go-getter" who is misguided and seeking harmful behaviors. When directed to healthy behaviors, the same go-getter becomes a hero and does amazing things."

The neural pathways for a digital media addiction are the same ones that are formed with addiction to drugs, sex, food, and even exercise. All these activities produce the same feel-good hormones and neurochemistry in the brain. When practiced to excess, these behaviors are destructive to the body, which is the temple of the Holy Spirit. Thus, all addictions are created equal because they share similar neurological and physiological pathways, as well as being sinful, and can prevent us from being physically and emotionally able to perform work needed to impact the Kingdom of GOD.

For all have sinned, and come short of the glory of God; Being justified freely by his grace through the redemption that is in Christ Jesus. - Romans 3: 23-24, KJV

We believe that GOD designed us with incredible drive, purpose, and "go-getter" attitude. So, a person struggling with addictive behaviors is really a "go-getter" who is misguided and seeking harmful behaviors. When directed to healthy behaviors, the same go-getter becomes a hero and does amazing things. We hear this often in people's personal testimonies. They were addicted to something or some behavior and then God heals them and they become a CEO of a major company or a church pastor. We should encourage one another in our battles with unhealthy behaviors that can lead to addiction, especially in the area of digital media addictions. Digital media addictions are one of the most difficult to overcome due to the necessity of them in our daily lives. People cannot just abstain from them as with other types of addictions. Perhaps with encouragement and not judgement, we will see more lives turned around and individuals doing amazing things.

Figure 8: Addiction Cycle. This is the model for addictive behaviors. Emotional triggers and stress lead to cravings for rituals of using something to relieve the stress. Excessive use leads to problems in life and then added guilt associated with ignoring relationships, important tasks, and self-care. The additional guilt results in more emotional triggers and stress. The entire cycle repeats over and over until the inciting emotional triggers and stress are resolved.

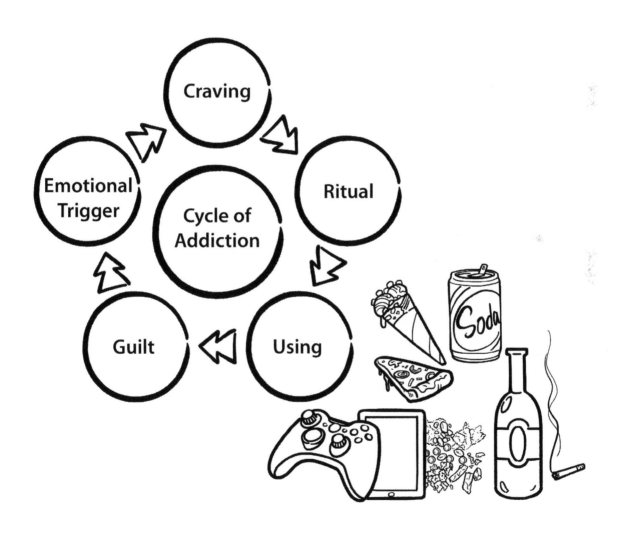

Points to consider and discuss:

1) Are some people more prone for addictive behaviors?

_____

_____

_____

_____

_____

2) Can people develop addictive behaviors later in life if exposed to addictive substances and addictive digital media during childhood?

_____

_____

_____

_____

_____

3) Why do we tend to abuse things that feel good?

_____

_____

_____

_____

_____

4) Improve this lesson by filling out the survey questions on page 73.

Lesson 8

40 Days to Healing

Then Jesus was led up by the Spirit into the wilderness to be tempted by the devil. And when He had fasted forty days and forty nights, afterward He was hungry.

- Matthew 4: 1-2, NKJV

All things are lawful for me, but all things are not helpful. All things are lawful for me, but I will not be brought under the power of any.

- 1 Corinthians 6: 12, NKJV

For those using this book at home, we recommend watching the videos on: www.realbattle.org/digital-vortex/, and then work through this lesson.

In the Bible, 40 days' time usually deals with judgment or testing and many scholars understand it to be the number of days for **probation** or trial. Rehab centers for addictions found that 30 to 40 days are helpful to assist people in their recovery. Dr. Victoria Dunckley in her book, "*Reset Your Child's Brain: A Four-Week Plan to End Meltdowns, Raise Grades, and Boost Social Skills by Reversing the Effects of Electronic Screen-Time*", also discovered that 30 or more days of digital screen removal helps with resolving behavioral and emotional problems in children. The 40 days are likely the time needed for healing of the mind and body and resetting the hormonal levels that are skewed due to excessive use and abuse. While we unplug from negative thoughts, avoid harmful behaviors, and addictions, our journey to better emotional and physical health starts with 40 days. During these 40 days, our mind clears and our hormonal levels reset to a new baseline as we practice self-discipline, restraint, and starving our senses. However, this may require more time depending on how long we have had the behavior we are seeking to change.

The difficulty of changing a habit depends on the individual and how long they have had the habit. The more repetition of the behavior, the stronger the neuronal pathways are for the behavior to stimulate the reward. Remember, neurons that fire together, wire together. In the 1960s, Dr. Maxwell Maltz published a book titled "*Psycho Cybernetics.*" He stated his observation that 21 days was the time it took for his patients to change a behavior. However, he never conducted any scientific study. The University College in London conducted a 12-week scientific study tracking 96 people and determined the average number of days to be 66 days for a new behavior to become a habit. Incidentally, the range was 18 days to 254 days. Thus, we recommend starting with 40 days to make a new healthy behavior into a habit. It may take longer, or it may never be possible to participate in some behaviors in a healthy manner. That is between each person and GOD to know what is healthy and acceptable to him. The Bible supports this in the verse:

> *"When we are rested and not overstimulated, even the simple pleasures give us incredible joy and excitement."*

"All things are lawful for me, but all things are not helpful. All things are lawful for me, but I will not be brought under the power of any." - 1 Corinthians 6: 12, NKJV

When we are rested and not overstimulated, even the simple pleasures give us incredible joy and excitement. This applies to our computer usage, nutrition, digital media and personal relationships. If we have fasted from sugar, and then have some to eat, we are sensitive to a small amount. If we have not used a video game for a few weeks and then play a game again, just a few minutes will be enough for us to feel the arousal and stimulation that was taking hours to achieve before the digital fast. By taking a break from highly stimulating activities, our brain is able to rest, reset and become sensitive to the pleasure derived from activities in our daily lives. As the brain resets its tolerance level, we do not need overstimulation from digital media to feel good. Because we are able to be more sensitive to less intense stimuli, we will desire face-to-face time and building personal relationships with our friends and family. Most importantly, we start to hear GOD's voice and discover joy in His plans for us. During the time unplugged from digital media, focus on healing and GOD.

Figure 9: Reward in Nature. As you unplug during camp or at home, look all around you and enjoy the beauty and amazing things in nature. As we admire GOD's work in nature, we develop a deep appreciation for His creativity, power, and love for us. We also stimulate our minds with feel good dopamine and hormones in the body as we marvel over His creations.

Points to consider and discuss:

1) Describe how you feel unplugging from digital devices.

_____

_____

_____

_____

_____

2) Are there behaviors that you desire to change or stop altogether?

_____

_____

_____

_____

_____

3) After the 40 days of unplugging, how will you develop and practice healthy behaviors?

_____

_____

_____

_____

_____

4) Improve this lesson by filling out the survey questions on page 73.

Lesson 9

Brain Pruning
Use It or Lose It!

He also spoke this parable: "A certain man had a fig tree planted in his vineyard, and he came seeking fruit on it and found none. Then he said to the keeper of his vineyard, 'Look, for three years I have come seeking fruit on this fig tree and find none. Cut it down; why does it use up the ground?' But he answered and said to him, 'Sir, let it alone this year also, until I dig around it and fertilize it. And if it bears fruit, well. But if not, after that you can cut it down.'"

– Luke 13: 6-9, NKJV

Train up a child in the way he should go, And when he is old he will not depart from it.

- Proverbs 22:6, NKJV

Let no one despise your youth, but be an example to the believers in word, in conduct, in love, in spirit, in faith, in purity.

- 1 Timothy 4:12, NKJV

For those using this book at home, we recommend watching the videos on:
www.realbattle.org/digital-vortex/, and then work through this lesson.

When we practice behaviors, the brain reinforces neuronal connections associated with these behaviors. Thus, the saying goes: neurons that fire together, wire together. There is another **neurological** process that relates to behavior called neural pruning or brain pruning. This is the process of the brain removing neuronal connections that are no longer used or useful in the brain and occurs around age 13 for the prefrontal cortex in the brain's frontal lobe. When we do not create the neuro-pathways because we do not practice certain behaviors, then we will lose access to the parts of the brain that are responsible for the behaviors. Therefore, if people under the age of 13 are not making neural connections in different parts of the brain, like learning self-discipline or forming friendships, those neuronal pathways are reduced or get shut down. Perhaps, that is why Proverbs 22:6 KJV says "Train up a child in the way he should go: and when he is old, he will not depart from it." Like the fig tree in Luke 13, good behaviors produce fruit in our lives. People can see the fruit as outcomes of the good behaviors we develop and practice. In the Luke 13 parable, bad behaviors and addictive behaviors fail to generate fruit. In this parable, Jesus recommends that after a certain time frame, if there is no fruit, then the tree may be too **dysfunctional** for recovery.

> *"As we cease destructive and harmful behaviors and we practice good behaviors, our brains will develop new neuronal connections."*

As we engage in behaviors, we must be careful not to practice destructive and harmful behaviors. The Bible teaches that with enough practice of bad behaviors, our lives may become too dysfunctional to repair. The concept "use it or lose it" can be applied to our ability to fulfill GOD's purpose for our lives. If we do not use the time, talents, and opportunities GOD puts in our lives because we are spending so much time on digital media or harmful behaviors, we might end up wasting so much time that GOD uses someone else for His work. And we lose our opportunity to experience GOD's work in our lives. However, do not lose hope. GOD is loving and forgiving. If we turn to Him and ask for help, then He will come to our aid. Jesus taught in Luke 13 that when we are willing to receive help, direction, and mentorship, then there is hope of bearing fruit in our lives. As we cease destructive and harmful behaviors and we practice good behaviors, our brains will develop new **neuronal connections**. The development of new neuronal connections is called plasticity, and neuronal plasticity occurs throughout life. As we age, it becomes more difficult to learn new behaviors, but with practice, determination, and GOD's help, all things are possible! So, do not lose hope.

The Bible is full of young heroes who did amazing things in very challenging times. David killed the giant Goliath in 1 Samuel 17 when he was in his teens. At a young age, Mary was the mother of Jesus in a time where she could have been killed for being pregnant out of wedlock. Jeremiah was a teen when he was called to be GOD's prophet. Daniel was a teen when he was forced to serve the king, yet he insisted that he abide by the rules of his faith even though he could have been killed. The young boy who selflessly gave his lunch to Jesus to feed the 5000 is another example of great faith. GOD is able to multiply their gifts no matter how small they may seem. Today is no different, there are young people faithfully doing great things all the time. So, don't feel like you are too young to be used by GOD! GOD can use your abilities and talents right now! As Timothy 4:12 states: Let no one despise your youth, but be an example to the believers in word, in conduct, in love, in spirit, in faith, in purity.

Figure 10: Fruitful Mind. When we apply what we learn in the Bible and ask Jesus into our lives, our brains are trained with healthy behaviors that manifest fruit, such as: focus, talents, empathy, communication skills, chastity, faithfulness, generosity, gentleness, goodness, joy, kindness, love, modesty, patience, peace, and self-control.

The Fruitful Mind

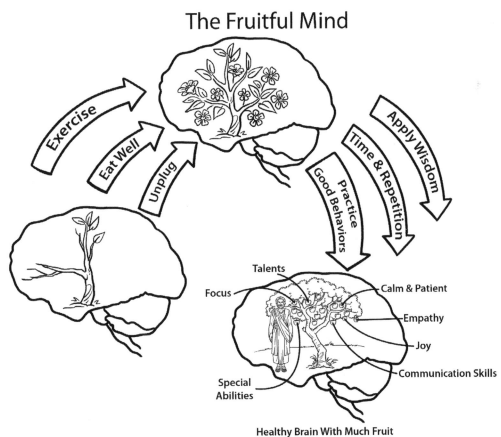

Healthy Brain With Much Fruit

Points to consider and discuss:

1) When is it best to start practicing good behaviors?

_____

_____

_____

_____

_____

2) What are examples of fruit in our lives as a result of good behaviors?

_____

_____

_____

_____

_____

3) Why are negative thoughts and harmful behaviors so destructive?

_____

_____

_____

_____

_____

4) Improve this lesson by filling out the survey questions on page 73.

Lesson 10

Stress Management

Casting all your care upon Him, for He cares for you.
-   1 Peter 5: 7, NKJV

Be anxious for nothing, but in everything by prayer and **supplication**, with thanksgiving, let your requests be made known to God; and the peace of God, which surpasses all understanding, will guard your hearts and minds through Christ Jesus.
- Philippians 4: 6-7, NKJV

Beloved, I pray that you may prosper in all things and be in good health, just as your soul prospers.
- 3 John1: 2, NKJV

Or do you not know that your body is the temple of the Holy Spirit who is in you, whom you have from God, and you are not your own? For you were bought at a price; therefore glorify God in your body and in your spirit, which are God's.
- 1 Corinthians 6: 19-20, NKJV

But his delight is in the law of the Lord And in His law he meditates day and night.
- Psalm 1: 2, NKJV

For those using this book at home, we recommend watching the videos on:
www.realbattle.org/digital-vortex/, and then work through this lesson.

The first step to healthy **stress management** is trusting in GOD and His love for us. GOD protects us in His hands, cares for us, and has wonderful plans for us. Regardless of our journeys on Earth, faith in Jesus Christ as our LORD and Savior ensures our salvation in Heaven. As GOD's children, we have won the eternal jackpot of entrance into Heaven! In Heaven, we will spend forever with GOD, our loving Father, and with our Christian family members and friends. Through Christ Jesus, we have a large family of brothers and sisters. Knowing GOD's love for us, plans for us in Heaven, and gift of salvation for us, we have courage and strength to face life difficulties.

> *"The first step to healthy stress management is trusting in GOD and His love for us. GOD protects us in His hands, cares for us, and has wonderful plans for us."*

If you have not received Jesus Christ as your LORD and Savior, then we invite you to do so now.

Pray this prayer used by Billy Graham who guided millions of people to Jesus:

Dear Lord Jesus, I know that I am a sinner, and I ask for Your forgiveness. I believe You died for my sins and rose from the dead. I turn from my sins and invite You to come into my heart and life. I want to trust and follow You as my Lord and Savior. In Your Name. Amen.

Practical Methods to Manage Stress

1) Take deep breaths when under stress. Controlled, deep breaths activate neuronal pathways in the brain associated with peace and calmness. These breaths will stimulate hormonal release to slow down the heart and hormones associated with calmness. When faced with fears, anxiety, and worries, clear your mind and take deep breaths. Ask the LORD for direction and wisdom. Philippians 4: 6-7 and Psalm 1:2.

2) Get physical exercise. Our bodies, mind, and soul benefit from regular exercise. We should aim for 30 minutes of exercise three to four times weekly. 3 John 1: 2 and 1 Corinthians 6: 19-20.

3) Get plenty of rest. One day of the week should be devoted to resting and recharging. The American Academy of Pediatrics recommends that teenagers 13 to 18 years of age should sleep 8 to 10 hours per 24 hours on a regular basis to promote optimal health. Getting 8 to 10 hours of sleep is essential for brain detoxification. Our brains get rid of toxins only when we sleep. Research has shown that sleep deprivation is like the physical effects of being drunk on two drinks of alcohol. Therefore, we can only be sober, wise, and make good judgements when we get adequate sleep.

4) Establish a sleep routine as outlined in Lesson 11.

5) Do not procrastinate. Make a list of urgent tasks and complete them in a timely fashion, with less stress.

6) Foster real, face-to-face relationships. Spend less time communicating with friends and family using digital media. Instead, spend face-to-face time with friends and family. When we spend face-to-face time, our brains are stimulated and hormones are released. This is why when we connect with people, we tend to get goose bumps and feel excited. Face-to-face encounters with people fill our brains with dopamine and the feel-good hormones necessary for resilience. Scientists refer to this experience with people as limbic resonance, where the brains of two people connecting seem to activate in similar areas together.

7) Eat healthy foods. Food is medicine and fuel for our bodies and mind. Garbage in will produce garbage out. Pick healthy foods to fuel your life and keep you able bodied. 1 Corinthians 6: 19-20.

Figure 11: Path to Peace. Jesus is the way, the truth, and the life. Jesus is the way to Heaven and stress free living. When struggling in life, realize that our time on Earth when compared to eternity is like a single grain of sand in all the oceans around the world. Our time on Earth is but a mere speck when compared to eternity. Every day, therefore, celebrate in your salvation and ticket to Heaven, a priceless gift from GOD for all those who have received Jesus as LORD and Savior!

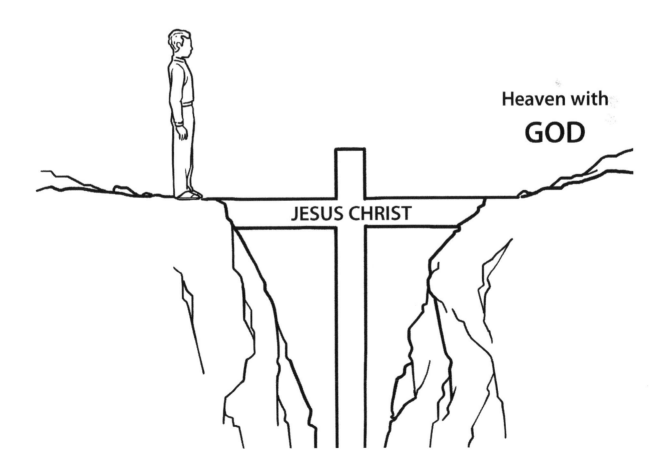

Points to consider and discuss:

1) Do digital media and digital devices prevent you from getting adequate sleep?

_____

_____

_____

_____

_____

2) How does digital media create more stress in your life?

_____

_____

_____

_____

_____

3) What are other methods you use to relieve stress?

_____

_____

_____

_____

_____

4) Improve this lesson by filling out the survey questions on page 73.

Lesson 11

Rest is Essential

And on the seventh day, God ended his work which he had made; and he rested on the seventh day from all his work which he had made. And God blessed the seventh day, and **sanctified** it: because that in it he had rested from all his work which God created and made.

- Genesis 2:2-3, KJV

It is vain for you to rise up early, To sit up late, To eat the bread of sorrows; for so He gives His beloved sleep.

- Psalm 127: 2, NKJV

For those using this book at home, we recommend watching the videos on:
www.realbattle.org/digital-vortex/, and then work through this lesson.

Even GOD rested on the seventh day after creating the Heavens and the Earth. If GOD rested, then it must be important. Sleep is just starting to be understood by science. Here are just 5 of the many functions our brain completes while it sleeps as outlined in the article by Carolyne Gregoire, *Healthy Living*:

1) Makes decisions.
2) Creates and organizes memories into recent information or long term memories.
3) Makes creative connections.
4) Learns and remembers how to perform physical tasks.
5) Clears out toxins.

During sleep, the harmful wastes from cellular **metabolism** are removed and **neutralized** by the brain. Sleep is essential to keeping our brains from becoming literally toxic! When our brains are toxic, we are more likely to make poor decisions, fall asleep in public settings and school, and more likely to be argumentative. When we rest, and set aside time to be unplugged, our minds can become bored. Boredom is a stimulus for creativity and for us to be able to hear GOD's Word. In the digital age, we are so busy and over-stimulated by entertainment that we are rarely bored. During sleep, our brains are very active. We often work out problems, come up with new ideas, and solidify what we have learned during sleep. This is why people often wake up with great ideas. Therefore, getting adequate sleep is essential to creativity and productivity.

> *"During sleep, our brains are very active. We often work out problems, come up with new ideas, and solidify what we have learned during sleep."*

Sleep hygiene is the set of practices performed that helps us develop habits that will give us quality nighttime sleep and maximize daytime alertness. Here are practical guidelines for healthy sleep hygiene.

Sleep Hygiene Tips

- Keep a regular schedule for bedtime, waking up and meal times. Routine keeps the inner body clock running smoothly.
- Time needed for sleep varies depending on age and the individual, but in general, teenagers will need 8 to 10 hours daily and adults need 7 to 9 hours daily.
- Avoid stimulants before bedtime, such as caffeine, candy, nicotine, and digital media. Avoid being stimulated by emotionally upsetting discussions or activities on social media, and in the home 1 to 2 hours before bedtime.
- Regular exercise is important to getting good sleep, but avoid exercising two hours before bedtime.
- Avoid rich food, fatty foods, spicy dishes, and carbonated drinks before bedtime.
- Unplug and wind down about 1 hour before bedtime. This means stop doing work 1 hour before laying down to sleep.
- Do not work in bed. If you cannot sleep, then work in an office or outside of the bedroom.

- Do not look at digital screens in the middle of the night. Turn off phone notifications, ringers, and social media notifications. Do not look at the light from the phone if awakened during the middle of the night. Light from the phone will tell the brain to prepare to start a new day.
- Get adequate exposure to natural sunlight during the day.
- Setup a regular relaxing bedtime routine and follow it every day, in the same order. A routine will help your body start the sleep process. This could be taking a warm shower, setting out your clothes for the morning, reading a book, or meditation with deep breathing.
- Make the sleep environment pleasant. The bed, pillow, and covers should be comfortable. The room should be cool. If necessary, use eye shades, ear plugs, white noise fan, humidifiers and other devices to make the room comfortable.

Figure 12: We Must Sleep! Adequate sleep is necessary for brain detoxification.

It is vain for you to rise up early, To sit up late, To eat the bread of sorrows; for so He gives His beloved sleep. - Psalm 127:2, NKJV

Points to consider and discuss:

1) Describe your moods when you're sleep deprived.

_____

_____

_____

_____

_____

2) Do you make good decisions when you're sleep deprived?

_____

_____

_____

_____

_____

3) Which activities and digital devices disrupt your sleep?

_____

_____

_____

_____

_____

4) Improve this lesson by filling out the survey questions on page 73.

Lesson 12
Unplug for Better Health

In the third year of the **reign** of Jehoiakim king of Judah, Nebuchadnezzar king of Babylon came to Jerusalem and **besieged** it. And the Lord gave Jehoiakim king of Judah into his hand, with some of the articles of the house of God, which he carried into the land of Shinar to the house of his god; and he brought the articles into the **treasure house** of his god. Then the king instructed Ashpenaz, the master of his **eunuchs**, to bring some of the children of Israel and some of the king's descendants and some of the nobles, young men **in whom there was no blemish**, but good-looking, gifted in all wisdom, possessing knowledge and quick to understand, who had ability to serve in the king's palace, and whom they might teach the language and literature of the Chaldeans. And the king appointed for them a daily provision of the king's delicacies and of the wine which he drank, and three years of training for them, so that at the end of that time they might serve before the king. Now from among those of the sons of Judah were Daniel, Hananiah, Mishael, and Azariah. To them the chief of the eunuchs gave names: he gave Daniel the name Belteshazzar; to Hananiah, Shadrach; to Mishael, Meshach; and to Azariah, Abed-Nego. But Daniel purposed in his heart that he would not **defile** himself with the portion of the king's delicacies, nor with the wine which he drank; therefore he requested of the chief of the eunuchs that he might not defile himself. Now God had brought Daniel into the favor and goodwill of the chief of the eunuchs. And the chief of the eunuchs said to Daniel, "I fear my lord the king, who has appointed your food and drink. For why should he see your faces looking worse than the young men who are your age? Then you would endanger my head before the king." So Daniel said to the steward whom the chief of the eunuchs had set over Daniel, Hananiah, Mishael, and Azariah, "Please test your servants for ten days, and let them give us vegetables to eat and water to drink. Then let our appearance be examined before you, and the appearance of the young men who eat the portion of the king's delicacies; and as you see fit, so deal with your servants." So he consented with them in this matter, and tested them ten days. And at the end of ten days their features appeared better and fatter in flesh than all the young men who ate the portion of the king's delicacies. Thus the steward took away their portion of delicacies and the wine that they were to drink, and gave them vegetables. As for these four young men, God gave them knowledge and skill in all literature and wisdom; and Daniel had understanding in all visions and dreams. Now at the end of the days, when the king had said that they should be brought in, the chief of the eunuchs brought them in before Nebuchadnezzar. Then the king interviewed them, and among them all none was found like Daniel, Hananiah, Mishael, and Azariah; therefore they served before the king. And in all matters of wisdom and understanding about which the king examined them, he found them ten times better than all the magicians and astrologers who were in all his realm. Thus Daniel continued until the first year of King Cyrus. - Daniel 1: 1-21, NKJV

For those using this book at home, we recommend watching the videos on:
www.realbattle.org/digital-vortex/, and then work through this lesson.

In the book of Daniel, the Jews were enslaved by Babylon. The King of Babylon, Nebuchadnezzar, asked for four teenage boys to be teachers and advisors to him. These young men were named Daniel, Shadrach, Meshach, and Abednego and equivalent to the best of the best teenage heroes amongst the Jewish people. When offered rich foods and wines by the king, the boys exhibited self-control and refrained from eating these foods and drinks. Eating herbs and vegetables and drinking water, they looked better, physically and emotionally, when compared to the king's servants who indulged with fine foods and drinks. In many ways, this scripture teaches us that the unhealthy habits of Babylon made the Babylonians slaves to their lavish lifestyle and overconsumption, entrapping them in their own folly. We don't want to be slaves to overconsumption in any area of our lives, even in digital media usage.

In the digital age, we have digital media that stimulate the mind and body similar to drugs. Based on research, we have evidence that the average American child is utilizing digital media for entertainment more than 7 hours daily (this does <u>not</u> include digital media associated with school and work). As our minds indulge in these activities, our brains do not develop other desired skills: communication, reading, writing, creativity, musical abilities, athletic skills, and much, much more. Remember, we need 10,000 hours of practice to develop proficiency in any skill. We become what we think and invest our time in. To find balance in the digital age, we recommend the following practical guidelines.

Healthy Tech Use Guidelines

- Limit digital media and gaming to less than one hour daily.
- Text less and call people instead (phone or video chat).
- Set aside time for daily exercise. Exercise at least 30 minutes, three to four times weekly.
- Spend face-to-face time with family and friends.
- Follow age restrictions on video games and movies. Therefore, mature video games are for those older than 17 years of age.
- Be aware of the signs and symptoms of digital media addiction. Seek help for your friends or yourself if there are problems. You will find more information at www.realbattle.org/resources/. People who are overusing digital media exhibit one or more of the following behaviors: poor emotional health, broken relationships, uncontrollable craving, using digital media to escape negative moods, withdrawal when removed from digital media, health problems, and financial difficulties.
- Encourage technology-free zones in our homes, such as the bedroom. Remove all digital screens or phones in the bedroom. The bedroom is for rest and sleep.
- No digital media for kids two and under, which are ages with critical brain development.
- Do not own smartphones until 14 years old or older. Use a flip phone without internet access instead. When our brains are under the age of 14, it is too difficult to have the self-control to resist being on the phones excessively. As our brains mature, we have more self-control and are better able to handle phones safely. We do not drive a car until age 16 in most countries. Therefore, we should not own smartphones until age 14 or older.

- Balance technology use with physical activities. For every hour of technology use, spend one hour of a physical activity.
- In your home, establish guidelines on technology storage and use a lock box if necessary.
- Stress management journaling, as discussed in the next chapter.

Figure 13: Digital Vortex.

Points to consider and discuss:

1) What other things or activities are similar to the fine foods and drinks in Daniel 1?

_____

_____

_____

_____

_____

2) Do we have to be clinically "addicted" to something to exhibit problems with the substance or behavior?

_____

_____

_____

_____

_____

3) What are other ways to unplug from digital media and maintain moderation with technology use?

_____

_____

_____

_____

_____

4) Improve this lesson by filling out the survey questions on page 73.

Conclusion

We have explored the factors motivating our behaviors, how the brain is programmed, and how we keep our brains healthy. Our brains make us who we are, and we should protect our brains by enabling their complete development. Taking steps to understand how neurochemistry works and limiting screen time can help a person achieve their full potential GOD has given them. Digital media, depending on the content and amount of usage, can be both good and bad. We encourage you to apply what you have learned in this workbook to your lives daily. With patience, practice, and repetition, you will train your brain to learn anything. With GOD, you are never alone and nothing is impossible.

Life is full of stress so it is important to learn how to manage stress. We all do this differently, so invest time to try different techniques to find what works for you. In order to figure out what works for you to manage stress, Helpguide.org suggests journaling. It does not have to be long entries. Just the act of writing a one word description of what is bothering you helps your mind cope with the stress in a healthy way. Here are topics to think about when you are stressed that will help you journal and develop mindfulness in a stressful time:

- Figure out what is causing stress for you.
- Think about how the stress made you physically feel and what emotions you experienced.
- What was your response to the stress?
- What did you do to make yourself feel better? Did your reaction help you or hurt you?

At first it may feel very strange to write in a journal, however with practice, it will get more natural. Then after a while of practicing the analytical skills you develop from journaling, you will be better equipped to handle stress. You will be able to analyze your feelings during stress. The stress you are feeling will diffuse and be more manageable. At the back of this workbook, we have included pages for you to journal.

> *"Unplug and live out GOD's plans for your life!"*

If you or someone you know feel the need for more help after completing this workbook, please consult a medical professional who is aware of digital media addictions.

Our website has medical professionals who work with digital media addictions:
http://realbattle.org/digital-detox-game-plan/

For additional educational resources and references, please visit here:
http://realbattle.org/resources/

Recommended books are listed on our website:
http://astore.amazon.com/medrounpublic-20

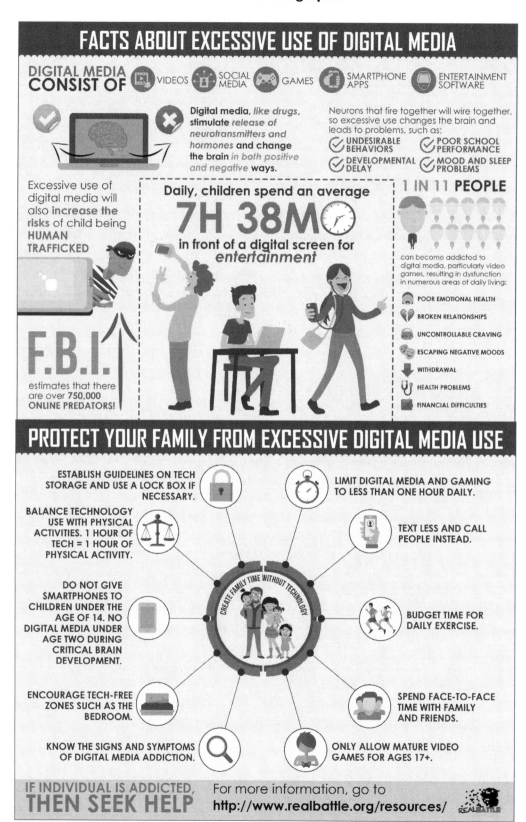

FACTS ABOUT EXCESSIVE USE OF DIGITAL MEDIA

DIGITAL MEDIA CONSIST OF VIDEOS · SOCIAL MEDIA · GAMES · SMARTPHONE APPS · ENTERTAINMENT SOFTWARE

Digital media, *like drugs,* **stimulate** *release of neurotransmitters and hormones* **and change the brain** *in both positive and negative* **ways.**

Neurons that fire together will wire together, so excessive use changes the brain and leads to problems, such as:
- UNDESIRABLE BEHAVIORS
- POOR SCHOOL PERFORMANCE
- DEVELOPMENTAL DELAY
- MOOD AND SLEEP PROBLEMS

Excessive use of digital media will also **increase the risks of child being HUMAN TRAFFICKED**

F.B.I. estimates that there are over **750,000 ONLINE PREDATORS!**

Daily, children spend an average **7H 38M** in front of a digital screen for *entertainment*

1 IN 11 PEOPLE can become addicted to digital media, particularly video games, resulting in dysfunction in numerous areas of daily living:
- POOR EMOTIONAL HEALTH
- BROKEN RELATIONSHIPS
- UNCONTROLLABLE CRAVING
- ESCAPING NEGATIVE MOODS
- WITHDRAWAL
- HEALTH PROBLEMS
- FINANCIAL DIFFICULTIES

PROTECT YOUR FAMILY FROM EXCESSIVE DIGITAL MEDIA USE

CREATE FAMILY TIME WITHOUT TECHNOLOGY

- ESTABLISH GUIDELINES ON TECH STORAGE AND USE A LOCK BOX IF NECESSARY.
- LIMIT DIGITAL MEDIA AND GAMING TO LESS THAN ONE HOUR DAILY.
- BALANCE TECHNOLOGY USE WITH PHYSICAL ACTIVITIES. 1 HOUR OF TECH = 1 HOUR OF PHYSICAL ACTIVITY.
- TEXT LESS AND CALL PEOPLE INSTEAD.
- DO NOT GIVE SMARTPHONES TO CHILDREN UNDER THE AGE OF 14. NO DIGITAL MEDIA UNDER AGE TWO DURING CRITICAL BRAIN DEVELOPMENT.
- BUDGET TIME FOR DAILY EXERCISE.
- ENCOURAGE TECH-FREE ZONES SUCH AS THE BEDROOM.
- SPEND FACE-TO-FACE TIME WITH FAMILY AND FRIENDS.
- KNOW THE SIGNS AND SYMPTOMS OF DIGITAL MEDIA ADDICTION.
- ONLY ALLOW MATURE VIDEO GAMES FOR AGES 17+.

IF INDIVIDUAL IS ADDICTED, THEN SEEK HELP

For more information, go to http://www.realbattle.org/resources/

REALBATTLE

Word Search from Lessons 1 and 2

```
U O V E R U S I N G W M I N E R A L N L
D D D S N O R U E N V U L N E R A B L E
R N N O S K O G T N E M E L E P E X P E
E U A D G S E L U C E L O M S Y O K E A
S W M L E S I T R E P X E C P G G A R P
O E H O L Y S P I R I T V E E S R M I R
L M P H S N O I S S I M N E E T G U O A
I E K V N Y Y P L A S T I C I T Y A D C
D N R E T T A M F O S E T A T S A R I T
D U E X Q J Z E V I T C I D D A Z T C I
T X C K H Q B C D V V X X Y L E E F T C
E P L I Q U I D H D E N U R P M S G A E
J X P V D R E P E T I T I O N U J P B Y
N O I T C E N N O C L A N O R U E N L Q
J F A I E L T T A B L A E R M U M V E P
V R X P S E N E G U R E H T A F J M N A
E N U I R T V B R A I N F U N C T I O N
W I S D O M I T H E A R M B I S G H I Q
H C H E M I C A L C O M P O U N D N H A
U E X E C U T I V E F U N C T I O N S Q
```

WORD LIST:

ADDICTIVE
BRAIN FUNCTION
CHEMICAL COMPOUND
DNA
ELEMENT
EXECUTIVE FUNCTIONS
EXPERTISE
FATHER
FEEL
GENES
HEAR
HOLY SPIRIT

LIQUID
MINERAL
MOLECULES
NEURONAL CONNECTION
NEURONS
OVERUSING
PERIODIC TABLE
PLASTICITY
PRACTICE
PRUNED
REAL BATTLE
REPETITION

SEE
SOLID
SON
STATES OF MATTER
TEEN MISSIONS
TRAUMA
TRIUNE
VULNERABLE
WISDOM
YOKE

Word Search from Lessons 3 and 4

```
E S U O R A Y F Z R R E C E P T O R S W
S N O T O H P T H G I L H U C C E T E I
D M O L E C U L A R A C T I O N B E S Q
A H S Y N A P S E K V G F C V X R T O L
N I V X V D S G N Z L P A Q T A I N G P
O A P A F N E Y O S A I G S F M D B S H
G A Q N P A V D I L N F E N U Y N S M O
N D P U I L R R T E L I N L T E A U M T
O R U G W G E U A E A N I I H N L M S O
I E T O G Y N N P P C I L B N I G A A R
T N H J I R C K I D I N E T I M L L E E
A A E V N A I E S E G O S E G A A A V C
L L E I G T T G S P O T A C Q P E H S E
U G R R E I P P I R L A B N G O N T E P
G L F D S U O N D I O L C A M D I O N T
E A H R T T N L D V I E B R Z L P P O O
R N C B W I F E B E S M I E L X U Y M R
S D E L C P I P D D Y T Q L J Q M H R S
Y S T I M U L A T E H W T O O K Y X O A
D R T Y U N P L U G P V S T F G S K H G
```

WORD LIST:

ADRENAL GLANDS
AROUSE
BASELINE
COCAINE
DISSIPATION
DOPAMINE
DRUNK
DYSREGULATION
GONADS
HORMONES

HYPOTHALAMUS
INGEST
LIGHT PHOTONS
MELATONIN
MOLECULAR ACTION
OPTIC NERVE
PHOTO RECEPTORS
PHYSIOLOGICAL
PINEAL GLAND
PITUITARY GLAND

RECEPTORS
SLEEP DEPRIVED
STIMULATE
STIMULI
SYNAPSE
TECHFREE
TOLERANCE
UNPLUG

Word Search from Lessons 5 and 6

```
A I B S D S M F S V S X K S F S U W Q X
J M J A I E X B T E L E S Y I Y M S R Q
E C D C G X N Z R N O E V T G A F T E L
S T Y R I E X N E T A T E H H W D I K K
N P S I T L H R N R T O M K T H E M N W
E R F F A F N E G A H L E A O T M U I Z
B E U I L E U P T L E E T D R A O L H L
M F N C M R J E H T S R A D F P T A T O
U R C E E K G T E E E A T I L D I T B N
C O T A D C O I N G L N I C I R V E M G
C N I D I I G T S M F C V T G A A H U T
A T O O A U N I T E C E A I H W T C H E
S A N P L Q I O G N O C R V T E E T T R
U L B A M E D N K T N C G E H R S T D M
E C O M M U N I C A T I O N S K I L L S
L O U I N L O W C L R V I R T U A L F F
C R Z N M Q B P I A O G I N D U L G E T
U T V E E A C M V R L M O T I V A T E D
N E V G S S T I F E N E B Y H T A P M E
A X Z S X V G N J A Q Y N E S O P R U P
```

WORD LIST:

ADDICTIVE
BENEFITS
BONDING
COMMUNICATION SKILLS
DEMOTIVATES
DIGITAL MEDIA
DOPAMINE
DYSFUNCTION
EMPATHY
FIGHT OR FLIGHT

GRAVITATE
INDULGE
LOATHES
LONG TERM
MOTIVATED
NUCLEUS ACCUMBENS
PREFRONTAL CORTEX
PURPOSE
QUICK REFLEXES
REPETITION

REWARD PATHWAYS
SACRIFICE
SELF CONTROL
STIMULATE
STRENGTHENS
THUMB THINKER
TOLERANCE
VENTRAL TEGMENTAL AREA
VIRTUAL

Word Search from Lessons 7 and 8

```
U D E I F I T S U J V I S U O L I R E P
M A N I F E S T H T W S D H E A L T H Y
F E N I L E S A B I A T S D N E I R F C
A I U E Y H D T O R D R F Z I Y C N A R
B T Y L T R C R Q I D E O M M O R M D E
L N L C E Y B E B R I N L I A J A R E W
E E I Y S S E G L P C G L S P N V E T A
B M M C E E R G G S T T Y G O S I S A R
O E A N R V I I O Y I H J U D E N T L D
D G F O S I W R G L O E T I A C G R U C
I A R I E T D T E O N N E D K I S A M Y
E N E T N P N L T H P H C E G O Y I I C
D A D C O A A A T F A E H D U H A N T L
C M E I M C E N E O T A F S L C D T S E
Y S M D R G R O R E H L A U L R Y R R V
E S P D O R I I S L W I S T I O T E E P
C E T A H J F T D P A N T I B O R S V X
A R I H V W I O M M Y G Q A L P O E O J
R T O J Q I M M W E J Y M R E F F T O Q
G S N O A K M E M T N E M E T I C X E E
```

WORD LIST:

ABLE BODIED
ADDICTION CYCLE
ADDICTION PATHWAY
BASELINE
CAPTIVES
CRAVING
DOPAMINE
EMOTIONAL TRIGGER
EXCITEMENT
FAMILY
FIRE AND WIRE
FOLLY

FORTY DAYS
FRIENDS
GOGETTERS
GRACE
GULLIBLE
HEALING
HEALTHY
HORMONES RESET
JOY
JUSTIFIED
MANIFEST
MISGUIDED

OVERSTIMULATED
PERILOUS
POOR CHOICES
REDEMPTION
RESET
RESTRAINT
REWARD CYCLE
STRENGTHEN
STRESS MANAGEMENT
TECH FAST
TEMPLE OF HOLY

Word Search from Lessons 9 and 10

```
G S S U C O F Y T I C I T S A L P L Q D
N D Y O J M U L T I P L Y G I F T S A G
I I L O V E S A L V A T I O N B C D N R
T V M E D I T A T E F R U I T F U L P E
S A S E I T I N U T R O P P O D K K A A
A D W N E U R O P A T H W A Y S T P T T
C N T N E M E G A N A M S S E R T S I F
R O I V A H E B D O O G E C A E P W E A
E N I T U O R Z J E R E M I A H A M N I
E C D N O I T I R T U N S L E E P Z C T
X O S H D T I E S O L R O T I E S U E H
E U Q H D Y N O I T A N I M R E T E D F
R R X E T R O C L A T N O R F E R P R P
C A S N O I T C E N N O C W E N N F T R
I G X B G E N E R A T E F R U I T I B A
S E S N S E O R E H G N U O Y A M A R Y
E H T A E R B P E E D T F N L E I N A D
W G N I N U R P H C H A L L E N G I N G
S T N E L A T V N Q L P R A C T I C E E
T L D E T O X S U P P L I C A T I O N Y
```

WORD LIST:

CASTING
CHALLENGING
COURAGE
DANIEL
DAVID
DEEP BREATH
DETERMINATION
DETOX
EXERCISE
FOCUS
FRUITFUL
GENERATE FRUIT
GOOD BEHAVIOR
GREAT FAITH

JEREMIAH
JOY
LOVE
MARY
MEDITATE
MULTIPLY GIFTS
NEUROPATHWAYS
NEW CONNECTIONS
NUTRITION
OPPORTUNITIES
PATIENCE
PEACE
PLASTICITY
PRACTICE

PRAY
PREFRONTAL CORTEX
PRUNING
ROUTINE
SALVATION
SLEEP
STRESS MANAGEMENT
SUPPLICATION
TALENTS
TIME
USE IT OR LOSE IT
YOUNG HEROES

Word Search from Lessons 11 and 12

```
W Y F T S E R L A I T N E S S E C W F D
M J O U R N A L S E L F C O N T R O L C
D S N O I T C E N N O C E V I T A E R C
E V E S M E L B O R P S E V L O S B G J
I M I N D F U L E C A F O T E C A F B H
F Q O R G A N I Z E S M E M O R I E S Z
I J L I M I T T E C H N E R O M K L A T
T E D A T I B K T E X T L E S S A E P M
C Z E D E Z I L A R T R U E N D B V N S
N Y T O D A I L Y E X E R C I S E Y E I
A L O G E D M F L I P P H O N E C W D L
S A X W G A L L E A R N S T A S K S X O
K N E A Y S R U O H T H G I E I D G J B
E A S T E N T H O U S A N D H O U R S A
O V E R C O N S U M P T I O N C L F D T
T Z C T X M A K E S D E C I S I O N S E
S T I B A H O T S E V A L S Z P H X L M
B S L E E P H Y G I E N E B A L A N C E
Y Y P G T E C H F R E E Z O N E Q U I P
C W C F K W T E C H L O C K B O X O E V
```

WORD LIST:

ANALYZE
BALANCE
CREATIVE CONNECTIONS
DAILY EXERCISE
DETOXES
EIGHT HOURS
EQUIP
ESSENTIAL REST
FACE TO FACE
FLIP PHONE

JOURNAL
LEARNS TASKS
LIMIT TECH
MAKES DECISIONS
METABOLISM
MINDFUL
NEURTRALIZED
ORGANIZES MEMORIES
OVERCONSUMPTION
SANCTIFIED

SELF CONTROL
SLAVES TO HABITS
SLEEP HYGIENE
SOLVES PROBLEMS
TALK MORE
TECH FREE ZONE
TECH LOCK BOX
TEN THOUSAND HOURS
TEXT LESS

Glossary

Adrenal Glands: These are endocrine glands that produce adrenaline and steroids aldosterone and cortisol. (wikipedia.org)

Astrology: The study of movements and relative positions of celestial bodies interpreted as having an influence on human affairs and the natural world. (Feedback.com)

Baseline: A basic standard or level; guideline; a specific value that can serve as a comparison or control. (Dictionary.com)

Besieged: Crowd around, surrounded. (Dictionary.com)

Casting: Throwing.

Chemical Compound: A thing that is composed of two or more separate elements; a mixture.

Cocaine: This is a powerfully addictive stimulant drug made from the leaves of the coca plant native to South America. Although health care providers use it for valid medical purposes, it is an illegal drug when not used by a doctor for medical purposes.

Cunning: Skill employed in a shrewd or sly manner, as in deceiving; craftiness; (Dictionary .com)

Defile: To make impure of unclean. (Merriam-Webster)

Digital Media: Digitized content that can be transmitted over internet or computer networks. (BusinessDictionary.com)

Dissipation: The action or process of self- indulgence, excessive drinking, and wasteful expenditure; dispersion, diffusion.

DNA: Deoxyribonucleic acid is a molecule that carries the genetic instruction used in the growth, development, functioning and reproduction of all known living organisms and many viruses. (Wikipedia)

Dopamine: This chemical acts as a messenger between brain cells. It helps control the brain's reward and pleasure centers. It also helps regulate movement and emotional responses. It enables us to see rewards and to take action to move toward them. (Sciencenewsforstudents.org)

Drunk: The condition of being in a temporary state in which one's physical and mental faculties are impaired by an excess of alcoholic drink; intoxicated. (Dictionary.com)

Dysfunction: The condition of having poor and unhealthy behaviors and attitudes within a group of people. (Merriam-Webster)

Element: Each of the more than one hundred substances that cannot be chemically broken down into simpler substances.

Endocrine System: The collection of glands that produce hormones that regulate metabolism, growth, and development, tissue function, sexual function, reproduction, sleep and mood. It is made up of the pituitary gland, thyroid gland, and parathyroid glands adrenal glands, pancreas, ovaries and testicles. (Live Science.com)

Eunich: A eunich was typically a slave who had been castrated in order to make them loyal servants for domestic duties.

Expedient: Fit or suitable for the purpose; proper under the circumstances. (Dictionary.com)

Expert: A person who has a comprehensive and authoritative knowledge of or skill in an area.

Expertise: The special skill or knowledge an expert has. (Dictionary. Com)

Folly: Lack of good sense, foolishness. (Feedback, Google)

Gene: A unit of heredity that is transferred from a parent to offspring and is held to determine some characteristic of the offspring. (Google Search)

Gonads: Sexual organs, such as the ovaries in females and testicles in males.

Gravitate: To move toward or be attracted to a place, person or thing. (Feedback, Google)

Gullible: Easily duped or cheated. (Merriam Webster)

Hormones: These are signaling molecules produced by glands in multicellular organisms that are transported by the circulatory system to target organs to regulate physiology and behavior. Hormones are essential for every activity of life, including the processes of digestion, metabolism, growth, reproduction and mood control. (Wikipedia and Medicinenet.com)

Hypothalamus: A region of the forebrain below the thalamus that coordinates both the autonomic nervous system and the activity of the pituitary, controlling body temperature, thirst, hunger, and other homeostatic systems, and involved in sleep and emotional activity. (Feedback- Google)

Hypothalamus-Pituitary-Adrenal Pathway: A complex set of direct influences and feedback interactions among the hypothalamus, pituitary gland, and adrenal glands. This is a neuroendocrine system that controls reactions to stress and regulates many body processes including digestion, mood, sleep, and immune system.

Indulge: To take unrestrained pleasure in: gratify. (Merriam-Webster)

Innate: Existing in one from birth; inborn; inherent in the essential character of something. (Dictionary.com)

Loatheth: Intense dislike or disgust for. (Feedback, Google)

Manifest: Display, show or demonstrate. (Feedback, Google)

Metabolize: To change food into a form that can be used by the body. (Merriam-Webster Dictionary)

Mineral: A solid inorganic substance of natural occurrence.

Molecule: This is an electrically neutral group of two or more atoms held together by chemical bonds. Molecules are different from ions because they lack an electrical charge.

Molecular Action: This is the biochemical interaction between molecules that produce an effect. (Wikipedia)

Neurological: Relating to the anatomy, functions and organic disorders of nerves and nervous system.

Neuron: A specialized cell that transmits nerve impulses. A nerve cell. (Feedback Google)

Neuronal Connections: Neurons become connected through the connection of neurons via dendrites and axons which enable signals to be sent and received between neurons. The signal between the axons of one neuron to the dendrite of the receiving neuron occurs at a structure known as a synapse. The process of the neurons sharing signals to perform a physical function such as hearing or vision requires "neuronal connections" to form so the brain can control physical functions. (Brain Facts. Org)

Neuronal Pathways: The same thing as neuronal connections.

Neurotransmitter: Chemical messenger in the brain. (Sciencenewsforstudents.org)

Neutralize: To stop someone or something from being effective or harmful. (Merriam-Webster)

Perilous: Full of danger or risk. (Feedback, Google)

Periodic Table of Elements: This is a tabular arrangement of the chemical elements, ordered by their number of protons, electron configurations and recurring chemical properties. This table is useful for analyzing chemical behavior and is widely used in chemistry and other sciences.

Photoreceptors: There are two types of photoreceptors contained in the back part of the eye (the retina). These are called rods and cones. There are about 120 million rods in a human retina. They are most sensitive to light and dark changes, shape and movement. There are about 6 million cones in the retina. Cones are most sensitive to green, red or blue colors. Signals form cones are sent to the brain to translate what color is being seen and they only work if there is light. (Faculty.washington.edu, Neuroscience for kids)

Photons: A photon is the fundamental particle of visible light. (whatis.techtarget.com/definition/photon)

Physiology: The branch of biology dealing with the functions and activities of living organisms and their parts, including all physical and chemical processes.

Physiological: Means of or relating to physiology. (Merriam-Webster)

Pituitary Gland: The pituitary gland is about the size of a pea and is situated in a bony hollow just behind the bridge of your nose. It is attached to the base of your brain by a thin stalk. The pituitary gland is often called the master gland because it controls several other hormone glands in your body, including the thyroid and adrenals, the ovaries and testicles. It has two parts: Front (anterior) lobe, which is 80% of its weight. Back (Posterior) lobe is 20% of its weight.

Pituitary Hormones: According to Merck Manual Consumer Version-
The 6 main hormones produced by the Anterior Pituitary Lobe are:
1. Growth hormone,
2. Thyroid-Stimulating Hormone,
3. Adrenocorticotropic hormone (ACTH) also called corticotrophin which stimulates the adrenal gland to produce cortisol and other hormones.
4. Follicle-stimulating hormone & luteinizing hormone (the gonadotropins which stimulate the sex organs to produce testosterone and estrogen)
5. Prolactin
6. Endorphins and enkephalins

The Posterior Pituitary Lobe Hormones are:
1. Vasopressin
2. Oxytocin

Probation: The process or period of testing or observing the character or abilities of a person in a certain role. (Feedback.com)

Pruning: To cut away.

Receptor: In biology, a receptor is a nerve ending that senses changes in light, temperature, pressure, etc., and causes the body to react in a way. (Merriam-Webster dictionary)

Reign: The period during which a sovereign or king occupies the throne. (Dictionary.com)

Reward Pathway: When activated by a rewarding stimulus (like food water or sex), information travels from the ventral tegmental area (VTA) to the nucleus accumbens, and up to the prefrontal cortex. This route through the brain is the reward pathway.

Ritual: A series of actions or behavior that is regularly followed by someone.

Sanctified: Set apart and declared holy. (Feedback, Google)

Slander: To male a false spoken statement that causes people to have a bad opinion of someone. (Merriam-Webster)

Sober: Not intoxicated or affected using alcohol, drugs, or other substances. (Free Dictionary)

Stimulate: Raise levels of physiological or nervous activity in the body or any biological system. Encourage interest or activity.

Stimuli: Things or events that evoke a specific functional reaction in an organ or tissue. (Feedback, Google)

Stress Management: This term refers to techniques to cope with stress for the purpose of improving daily functioning. (Wikipedia)

Supplication: An honest, humble request. (Merriam-Webster)

Synthesize: To form by combining parts. To combine into a single or unified entity. (Dictionary.com)

Tolerance: A state in which an organism no longer responds to a drug, so a higher dose is required to achieve the same effect. (National Institute of Health/ drugabuse.gov)

Trauma: Serious injury to the body, as from physical violence or an accident. Severe emotional or mental distress caused by an experience. (The Free Dictionary)

Vessel: A container for holding something.

Vulnerable: Able to be easily physically, emotionally, or mentally hurt, influence, or attacked. (Cambridge English Dictionary)

Womb: Uterus; place where something is begun or developed. (Merriam-Webster)

Personal Journal

_____

_____

_____

_____

_____

_____

_____

_____

_____

_____

_____

_____

_____

_____

_____

_____

_____

DIGITAL VORTEX SURVIVAL GUIDE - SURVEY

To help us assess and improve, please complete this survey on some of the key topics. Read the statement and mark the column that fits most closely with your opinion. When complete, please return it to your team leader or take a photo with your phone and e-mail to gamefreehome4u@gmail.com Thank you!

Lesson #	Statement	Strongly Agree	Agree	Neutral	Disagree	Strongly Disagree
1	This lesson gave biblical & scientific support to validate GOD is Real.					
1	The figures in this lesson illustrated the concepts of God being Real, Triune, and partnered with us.					
2	I understand how experience forms neuronal pathways.					
2	I am confused by the concept that my brain will "prune" itself.					
2	My brain needs to fully develop through age 25, when pruning is complete.					
3	Neurotransmitters are the chemical messengers that enable my brain to control my body, allow for learning, and create emotions.					
3	What I see, feel, smell, hear, and taste are the signals that stimulate the brain's reward pathway.					
3	I would like more explanation about the neuron cell and how it works so this lesson makes more sense to me.					
4	The optic nerve stimulates powerful brain chemistry from light.					
4	The bright light from a digital media device's screen can disrupt my sleep cycle and lead to hormonal problems and depression.					
4	I don't understand the lesson concepts and need more explanation.					
5	My brain is designed to seek rewards.					
5	Spending more than two hours a day on digital media could cause me to NOT develop areas of my brain that are important to my life.					
5	After age 14 my brain stops learning new things.					
6	Tolerance to dopamine will require me to spend more time and seek more extreme activities to feel the same pleasure.					
6	I understand where dopamine comes from in my brain.					
7	Poor stress management can lead to addiction.					
7	Addiction to drugs, food, gambling, exercise, and digital media all stimulate the same reward pathway that produce the same neurotransmitter called dopamine.					
7	I am confused about the cycle of addiction.					
8	By taking a break from digital media for 40 days, my brain will rest and need less stimulation to feel good.					
8	My baseline hormone levels can be reset and make life more interesting.					
8	Overstimulated brains are not healthy.					
9	Plasticity is the brain's ability to learn new things.					
9	If I don't use my mind to learn while I am young, my brain will not be productive.					
9	The Bible illustration of the fruitful tree was helpful.					

Lesson #	Statement	Strongly Agree	Agree	Neutral	Disagree	Strongly Disagree
10	It was helpful to suggest that our salvation is a key tool to managing stress.					
10	The practical tips for stress management were easy to understand.					
11	My digital screen could cause me to NOT sleep well if I use it too close to bedtime.					
11	Sleep makes no difference to my health.					
12	My body is a machine that needs to be given rest, healthy food, exercise, and education.					
12	We practice what we become.					
General	I am motivated to set healthy digital media usage times to less than 1 hour per day.					
General	Young people are today's heroes!					
General	I am confused about the science presented in this workbook.					
Glossary	I used the Glossary often to find the definitions for words that I did not understand. The Glossary was very helpful.					
General	I use digital media devices – including games, smart phone, social media – between 10 and 20 hours per week.					
General	I use digital media devices – including games, smart phone, social media – more than 20 hours per week.					
General	Thanks to these lessons, I plan on making positive changes in my life and reducing my use of digital media.					
General	These lessons were easy to understand.					
	My Additional Comments:					

Name: _____ **(optional)**

What is your age in years......12, 13, 14, 15, 16, 17, 18, 19, 20 or _____?

What grade level of education have you completed?   6th,   7th,   8th,   9th,   10th,   11th,   12th   College

Circle your gender: Male   Female

What science classes have you completed?
   1)   General science 7th grade
   2)   Health Education
   3)   Biology
   4)   Chemistry
   5)   Physics
   6)   Advanced Placement Chemistry
   7)   Advanced Placement Biology

Would you like to be on our email list for more information regarding digital media use?

Yes: _____.   My email address: _____

No thank you: _____.

Made in the USA
San Bernardino, CA
01 June 2017